500 RECIPES FOR
SUPPERS AND SNACKS

500 RECIPES FOR SUPPERS AND SNACKS

by Marguerite Patten

HAMLYN

Cover photograph by Paul Williams

Published by Hamlyn Publishing
Astronaut House, Feltham, Middlesex, England

First published 1963
Revised edition 1971
Fifteenth impression 1985

ISBN 0 600 37956 6

Printed and bound in Great Britain by
R. J. Acford

Contents

Introduction

This book has been written to provide recipes for light dishes and snacks that are just right for supper, luncheon or any time when you need a satisfying dish, which is not too heavy and which is quick to prepare.

During the past years most families have tended to avoid two heavy meals during the day, so that after a substantial meal only a light supper is required. On the other hand, should you have your family meal in the evening, then you will want a lunch which is not too heavy.

Some of the recipes in this book, however, can – by adding extra vegetables, etc. – be made into a really good main dish should the occasion arise.

In view of the popularity of television and the fact that many people have their meal while watching it, I have selected quite a number of the recipes so that they are not only pleasant to eat, but are easy to manipulate on an armchair tray.

Some Useful Facts and Figures

Notes on metrication

In case you wish to convert quantities into metric measures, the following tables give a comparison.

Solid measures

Ounces	Approx. grams to nearest whole figure	Recommended conversion to nearest unit of 25
1	28	25
2	57	50
3	85	75
4	113	100
5	142	150
6	170	175
7	198	200
8	227	225
9	255	250
10	283	275
11	312	300
12	340	350
13	368	375
14	396	400
15	425	425
16 (1 lb)	454	450
17	482	475
18	510	500
19	539	550
20 (1¼ lb)	567	575

Note: When converting quantities over 20 oz first add the appropriate figures in the centre column, then adjust to the nearest unit of 25. As a general guide, 1 kg (1000 g) equals 2·2 lb or about 2 lb 3 oz. This method of conversion gives good results in nearly all cases, although in certain pastry and cake recipes a more accurate conversion is necessary to produce a balanced recipe.

Liquid measures

Imperial	Approx. millilitres to nearest whole figure	Recommended millilitres
¼ pint	142	150
½ pint	283	300
¾ pint	425	450
1 pint	567	600
1½ pints	851	900
1¾ pints	992	1000 (1 litre)

Oven temperatures

The table below gives recommended equivalents.

	°C	°F	Gas Mark
Very cool	110	225	¼
	120	250	½
Cool	140	275	1
	150	300	2
Moderate	160	325	3
	180	350	4
Moderately hot	190	375	5
	200	400	6
Hot	220	425	7
	230	450	8
Very hot	240	475	9

Notes for American and Australian users

In America the 8-oz measuring cup is used. In Australia metric measures are now used in conjunction with the standard 250-ml measuring cup. The Imperial pint, used in Britain and Australia, is 20 fl oz, while the American pint is 16 fl oz. It is important to remember that the Australian tablespoon differs from both the British and American tablespoons; the table below gives a comparison. The British standard tablespoon, which has been used throughout this book, holds 17·7 ml, the American 14·2 ml, and the Australian 20 ml. A teaspoon holds approximately 5 ml in all three countries.

Meals on a Tray

There are a number of recipes in this book which are suitable to serve on a tray or eaten with just a fork, but this chapter contains dishes that are particularly easy to manage. When planning fireside trays, the food will look more interesting if it is cooked in individual portions. Where one main dish is given you may like to divide it into serving portions before cooking and, of course, it will take less time to cook this way.

When serving fish dishes for television snacks, be ultra careful about removing bones since the half light could cause a serious accident, particularly in the case of elderly or the younger members of your family.

Do not try and balance too many dishes on the tray at one time. It is easier to have the next course waiting in the kitchen or on a side table or trolley ready to be served.

Fish cakes

cooking time: 10 minutes, plus time in cooking potatoes and fish

you will need:

8 oz. mashed potatoes	1 egg
8 oz. cooked fish	salt
(cod, hake or other white fish)	pepper

to coat:

flour	crisp breadcrumbs
1 egg	

to fry: 2 oz. lard or oil

1 Put the well mashed potatoes into a basin.
2 Add the fish and mix thoroughly with a fork.
3 Add the beaten egg, salt and pepper.
4 Form into about 8 flat round cakes.
5 Roll these cakes in a little flour, then brush lightly with beaten egg and coat with breadcrumbs. Pat well to remove excess crumbs.
6 Heat the fat in a frying pan and when a faint haze is seen, fry quickly on one side and then the other.
7 Drain on crumpled tissue paper for about 2 minutes in a warm place and serve at once.

Variations

Fish and shrimp cakes – add 2 oz. chopped shrimps or chopped prawns.

Fish and tomato cakes – bind with the pulp of 2 or 3 skinned tomatoes instead of egg.

Tuna fish cakes – bind the contents of a medium can of tuna fish with the potatoes, add a little of the tuna liquid from the can and the beaten egg. This can be flavoured with chopped parsley and chopped chives.

Using a white sauce – many people prefer to bind the cakes with a thick white sauce made from 1 oz. margarine, 1 oz. flour and $\frac{1}{4}$ pint milk. Use this instead of the egg in the fish cakes in this case.

Economical fish cakes – to be more economical you could use $\frac{1}{2}$ egg in mixing the fish cakes and the other half for brushing them on the outside.

Salmon fish cakes – use either canned salmon or cooked fresh salmon.

With gherkin or cucumber – for an unusual sharp flavour, add a little finely chopped gherkin or cucumber to the fish and potato mixture.

New flavourings for fish cakes

Curried fish cakes – fry a teaspoon of chopped onion in a little butter or margarine, then work in a teaspoon curry powder, and add to the other ingredients.

Devilled fish cakes – fry a teaspoon chopped onion in a little butter or margarine, then add $\frac{1}{2}$ teaspoon curry powder, $\frac{1}{2}$ teaspoon Tabasco sauce and a few drops chilli sauce if wished. Add this mixture to the other ingredients.

To make a tray meal – arrange the fish cakes on hot plates and garnish with chopped parsley. Do not serve wedges of lemon, since these are difficult to handle on a tray, but squeeze a little lemon juice over the fish cakes just before serving.

Serve with either small wedges of tomato and shredded lettuce in a crisp salad or with fried sliced mushrooms, fried sliced tomatoes, and creamed spinach.

Tomato sauce or tartare sauce are also good accompaniments (see page 84).

Fish croquettes

cooking time: 10 minutes

Use any of the recipes for fish cakes (see page 9) but instead of mashed potato, bind with 2–3 oz. fine soft breadcrumbs, beating these with the fish until smooth.

The croquettes can be moistened with either the egg or with a thick white sauce made from:

1 oz. butter or margarine	¼ pint milk or partly milk and partly fish stock
1 oz. flour	
salt and pepper	

1 Bind the mixture together thoroughly, and if it is a little soft, allow it to stand in a cool place before handling.
2 Although it is correct to form croquettes into finger shapes these really need a good depth of fat to fry them evenly, so you can form them into flatter cakes like fish cakes instead.
3 Fry in the same way as fish cakes (see page 9).

Fish and rice croquettes (1)

cooking time: 30 minutes

you will need:

2 oz. rice* uncooked	12 oz. white fish
salt and pepper	1 egg

to coat:

flour	crisp breadcrumbs
1 egg	

to fry:

fairly deep fat or oil

*if possible use a medium grain rice

1 Put the rice into a saucepan with ¼ pint water and a good pinch of salt.
2 Bring to the boil, stir briskly, and put a very tightly fitting lid over the rice. Reduce the heat and cook for 14 minutes until the rice is soft.
3 Do not remove the lid during this period.
4 While the rice is cooking put the fish into a little cold water with seasoning and simmer steadily until soft.
5 Drain the fish well, remove skin and bones, and flake.
6 Mix with the cooked rice, which should require no draining, since it should have absorbed all the water. If not, drain very well.
7 Blend thoroughly with the beaten egg and seasoning.

8 Allow mixture to stand till cool before forming into finger shapes.
9 Coat with flour, then with beaten egg and crumbs.
10 Fry steadily until crisp and golden brown in the hot fat.
11 Drain on absorbent paper and serve hot or cold.

Variations

Anchovy rice croquettes

1 Pound about 8 anchovy fillets with the cooked fish. Be sparing with salt.
2 Blend ½–1 teaspoon anchovy essence with the egg. Be sparing with salt.

Haddock rice croquettes – use smoked haddock instead of white fish.

Tuna rice croquettes – use a large can tuna fish (drained) instead of cooked white fish.

Salmon rice croquettes – use a medium or large can red or pink salmon (drained) instead of cooked white fish.

To make a tray meal – as a contrast to the crisp texture of the croquettes, serve creamed spinach and a cheese, tartare or parsley sauce (see pages 83, 84).

The rice really takes the place of potatoes, but for a more sustaining supper add creamed potatoes or sauté potatoes.

Any salads are good with these croquettes, particularly a coleslaw (see page 58).

Bacon baps

cooking time: 15 minutes

you will need:

¾ oz. yeast	½ teaspoon salt
1 level teaspoon sugar	1–1½ oz. lard or cooking fat
just under ⅓ pint milk and water	milk for brushing
12 oz. plain flour	extra flour to dust baps

filling:

bacon, tomatoes

1 Cream the yeast and sugar together in a bowl.
2 Warm the liquid to blood heat and pour over the yeast.
3 Sieve flour and salt and rub in the lard.
4 Make a well in the centre of the mixture and pour in the yeast liquid.

5 Leave in a warm place for about 15 minutes until the yeast liquid is covered with little bubbles.

6 Knead dough until you leave the mixing bowl clear and have a smooth ball of dough.

7 Cover with a cloth so the outside does not harden and put to 'prove' in a warm place for approximately 1 hour.

8 Knead again and form into oval shapes.

9 Put on to warm and greased baking tins – allowing space for the baps to rise and spread.

10 Brush with a little milk and dust with flour.

11 Leave to 'prove' again for approximately 15 minutes in a warm place.

12 Dust with a little more flour before baking and press the tops firmly to keep a smooth surface.

13 Bake for approximately 15 minutes in a hot oven (425–450°F. – Gas Mark 7).

14 Fill with fried or grilled rashers of bacon.

To make into a tray meal – serve hot with a crisp green salad. Split baps through the centre and top with diced fried bacon and sliced fried tomatoes to add colour.

Variation

Kidney baps – skin, core and quarter 4 lamb's kidneys. Melt about 2 oz. butter and lightly fry one small chopped onion, add kidneys. Cook until soft. Blend 1 level teaspoonful of curry powder with 1 tablespoon Worcestershire sauce. Add to the kidneys and mix in 2–3 drops Tabasco sauce. Pile inside cooked baps.

Bengal canapés

cooking time: 15–25 minutes

you will need:
for sauce:

1 oz. margarine	seasoning
½ oz. cornflour or 1 oz. flour	4 slices bread chutney
¼ pint milk	2 tablespoons grated cheese
2 tablespoons cream	parsley
4 oz. cooked ham, diced	

1 Make the thick white sauce with margarine, cornflour and milk.

2 Add cream, ham and seasoning.

3 Toast or fry the bread and spread with the chutney, then the ham mixture.

4 Cover with the grated cheese and brown under the grill or in a moderately hot oven.

5 Garnish with parsley and more chutney if liked.

To make a tray meal – serve with grilled or baked tomatoes, creamed spinach, or grilled mushrooms.

Hamburgers

cooking time: 15–30 minutes

you will need:

1 large potato, peeled	pinch mixed herbs seasoning
8 oz. minced beef	crisp breadcrumbs
1 medium sized onion	little fat for frying or grilling
1 teaspoon Worcestershire sauce	
1 dessertspoon chopped parsley	

1 Grate the potato and mix with all the other ingredients except breadcrumbs.

2 Add no extra liquid as the potato keeps the mixture moist.

3 Form into rounds and roll in crisp breadcrumbs.

4 Bake on a greased tin in a moderately hot oven (400°F. – Gas Mark 5) for 30 minutes.

5 Alternatively, grill for 15 minutes, turning after 5 minutes, or fry, using only enough fat to cover the bottom of the pan.

To make a tray meal – serve with crisp salads. A rice salad (see page 58) is excellent, or serve with grilled or fried mushrooms, tomatoes (both cut into convenient small sized pieces for ease of management) and creamed potatoes.

Variety with hamburgers

The basic recipe for hamburgers is given above, but this can be varied in a number of ways:

Oatmeal hamburgers – add a good tablespoon rolled oats instead of the grated potato.

Egg hamburgers – omit the potato and bind with beaten egg.

Herb hamburgers – mix a good teaspoon of freshly chopped herbs, e.g. thyme, sage, mint, with the meat mixture.

Note

When you have not time to make your own hamburgers remember that you can buy a similar product frozen, and occasionally in cans. These can be substituted in any of the following recipes.

Fried hamburgers with mustard

cooking time: 15–30 minutes

1 Make hamburgers as before.
2 Spread hamburgers with made mustard.
3 Coat with flour and breadcrumbs.
4 Fry in hot fat until crisp and brown on both sides.
5 Serve with vegetables or salad.

Hamburgers with bananas and tomato sauce

cooking time: 15–30 minutes

1 Make hamburgers as before, brush with a little hot fat and grill or fry.
2 Place on a hot dish.
3 Fry banana slices in a little hot butter.
4 Serve with boiled rice and tomato sauce (see page 84), or condensed tomato soup which makes an excellent quick sauce.

Hamburgers with mushrooms and bacon

cooking time: 15 minutes

1 Make hamburgers as before and fry in a little hot fat, or brush with fat and grill.
2 At the same time, grill or fry sliced mushrooms and diced bacon until crisp and golden.
3 Top each hamburger with the mushroom and bacon mixture.
4 Serve with vegetables, bread or toast.

Tomatoburgers with onion

cooking time: 15 minutes

1 Make hamburgers, and grill or fry in a little hot fat.
2 At the same time, grill or fry thick slices of well seasoned tomato.
3 Top the hamburgers with the tomato slices and serve with fried onions.
4 If liked, the slices of uncooked tomato can be sandwiched between 2 thin hamburgers and cooked inside the meat.

Hamburgers with rice and barbecue sauce

cooking time: 35 minutes

1 Make hamburgers (see page 11) and fry in a little fat or brush with fat and grill.

2 Serve with boiled rice and barbecue sauce (see page 27).

Hamburgers on skewers

cooking time: 15–30 minutes

1 Make hamburgers (see page 11).
2 Cut hamburgers into cubes.
3 Thread on to metal skewers with cubes of apple, pieces of small onions, cubes of bacon, small mushrooms and tomatoes.
4 Allow 1 skewer per person for a light snack, 2 skewers for a more substantial meal.
5 Brush all the ingredients with a little melted butter.
6 Cook steadily under a grill or in a moderately hot oven (400°F. – Gas Mark 5) until all the ingredients are cooked.

Burger fritters

cooking time: 10 minutes

you will need:
ingredients as for hamburgers (see page 11).

for batter:

4 oz. plain flour	$\frac{1}{4}$ pint milk
pinch salt	2 tablespoons water
1 egg	fat for deep frying

1 Make hamburgers.
2 Make the batter in the usual way.
3 Dip each hamburger into the batter and cook in hot fat until crisp and golden brown.
4 Serve with green salad.

Variations
Tomatoburger fritters – use recipe above, but instead of milk in the batter use tomato juice.
Cheeseburger fritters – use recipe above, but add 1–2 oz. grated cheese to the batter.

Hamburger and tomato casserole

cooking time: 50 minutes

you will need:

1 lb. mixed vegetables	Ingredients as for
$\frac{1}{4}$ pint tomato sauce,	hamburgers (see
or can condensed	page 11)
tomato soup	

1 Cut the vegetables into cubes or slices.
2 Put into a casserole and cover with the tomato sauce or diluted tomato soup.

3 Cover the casserole with foil or a lid and cook for approximately 25 minutes in a moderate oven (375°F. – Gas Mark 4).

4 Make the hamburgers and arrange them on top of the vegetables and tomato mixture.

5 Return to the oven for a further 20–25 minutes.

Variation

With cooked vegetables – if using cooked vegetables, heat these for 10 minutes in the tomato sauce, add the hamburgers and heat for a further 20–25 minutes.

French bread and hamburger mornay

cooking time: 20 minutes

you will need:

ingredients as for hamburgers (see page 11)

French bread	made mustard
butter	Gruyère or Cheddar
1 onion, chopped	cheese, sliced
finely **or**	
chives, chopped and	
tomato ketchup or	

1 Make hamburgers.

2 Cut fairly thick slices of French bread and cover with butter, finely chopped onion or chives and tomato ketchup or made mustard.

3 Put a hamburger on each piece of bread and cover with slices of Gruyère or Cheddar cheese.

4 Grill steadily until hot and the cheese has melted.

5 Serve with grilled tomatoes and mushrooms or with a green salad.

Variation

Using toast – toast can be used instead of French bread if preferred and the cheese can be placed under the hamburger.

Hamburgers with apple and curry sauce

cooking time: 12–25 minutes

you will need:

ingredients as for hamburgers (see page 11)

2 cooking or	Patna rice, boiled
dessert apples	curry sauce
butter, melted	

1 Core apples and peel if wished. Cut into 6 slices.

2 Sandwich the apple slices in between 2 hamburgers.

3 Brush with melted butter and grill SLOWLY to cook the apple as well as the hamburgers.

4 Turn when one side is golden brown.

5 If preferred, the hamburgers and apple slices can be cooked in a hot oven (425°F. – Gas Mark 6) for approximately 25 minutes.

6 Serve with boiled rice and curry sauce.

Curry sauce

cooking time: 25 minutes

you will need:

1 oz. margarine	½ pint stock or ½ pint
1 small onion,	water with bouillon
chopped	cube
1–2 level teaspoons	little seasoning
curry powder	pinch sugar
2 level teaspoons	1 teaspoon concen-
flour	trated tomato paste

1 Heat the margarine in a pan, stir in the onion and cook for several minutes.

2 Gradually blend in the curry powder and flour and continue cooking with the onion for about 3 minutes.

3 Add the liquid, bring to the boil and cook until the mixture thickens.

4 Add the seasoning, sugar and tomato paste and simmer for 10 minutes.

Variation

With chutney and dried fruit – chutney, a tablespoon dried fruit, or a little coconut can all be added if wished and the amount of curry powder can be increased to taste.

Pineappleburger 'top hats'

cooking time: 15 minutes

you will need:

4 soft rolls or 8	4 hamburgers (see
rounds bread	page 11)
butter	4 pineapple rings
little made mustard	sprinkling brown sugar

1 Split the rolls through the centre and toast lightly on both sides.

2 Spread with butter and a little mustard and keep hot.

3 Brush the hamburgers and pineapple slices with a little melted butter.

4 Cook until golden coloured, sprinkling the pineapple with sugar if wished.

5 Place hamburgers and pineapple rings between toasted rolls.

Spiced ham balls

cooking time: 15–20 minutes

you will need:

8 oz. boiled bacon or ham	4 oz. soft fairly fresh breadcrumbs

for sauce:

1 oz. butter	1 tablespoon
1 oz. flour	Worcestershire
¼ pint milk	sauce
1–2 teaspoons tomato ketchup	seasoning

for coating:

1 egg	OR 2–3 oz. rather
crisp breadcrumbs	dry cheese, finely
fat for frying	grated
	OR already toasted crumbs

1 Chop ham very finely and mix with the crumbs.
2 Make a white sauce with butter, flour and milk.
3 Add ketchup, Worcestershire sauce and plenty of seasoning.
4 Add to the ham and crumbs while still hot.
5 Mix very thoroughly together.
6 Allow to cool and shape into tiny balls.
7 If you wish to fry these and give them a crisp coating, then brush with beaten egg, roll in crumbs and fry, or roll in the cheese or toasted crumbs but do not cook.

To make into a tray meal – serve with crisp salads or with a cheese flavoured creamed potato border.

Torpedoes

cooking time: 15–20 minutes

you will need:

8 oz. minced cooked meat	¼ pint thick white sauce or onion white
1 tablespoon chopped parsley	sauce (see page 83)
	1 Vienna loaf
	2 tomatoes

1 Add the minced meat and parsley to the sauce.
2 Split the loaf in half lengthwise and spread each half with the meat mixture.
3 Peel and slice the tomatoes and arrange on top.
4 Wrap each half in foil and bake in a moderate oven (375°F. – Gas Mark 4).

To make into a tray meal – unwrap the stuffed loaf, then cut into convenient sized fingers. If preferred, insert a palette knife through the centre, so that the stuffing is evenly spread on each half of the loaf, then cut into easy to manage fingers. Serve with watercress or lettuce.

Lettuce roll

no cooking

you will need:

½ lettuce	1 tablespoon grated
1 large or 2 small tomatoes	cheese
seasoning	few drops salad dressing

1 Wash lettuce and dry leaves well.
2 Put two of the largest leaves on the table as the outer part of the salad.
3 Skin tomato and cut into very thin slices. Add seasoning and grated cheese.
4 Put this mixture into the centre of the lettuce leaf, adding a very small amount of salad dressing.
5 Put smaller leaves over the top then roll, as though you were making a Swiss roll.
6 You may find it necessary to break the stalk up the back of the leaves so they do not come unrolled. (1 serving)

To make into a tray meal – serve after a fairly sustaining soup, choose one that includes fish, meat or plenty of vegetables, but not cheese.

Fish and lettuce roll

no cooking

you will need:

½ lettuce	2 teaspoons Parmesan
1 teaspoon horse-radish cream	cheese
seasoning	2 teaspoons finely chopped cucumber
4 oz. cooked or canned fish	or gherkin

1 Wash lettuce and dry leaves well.
2 Select largest leaves and place two on the table as the outer part of the salad.
3 Mix all other ingredients together, stirring until they form a smooth mixture that is not likely to crumble or fall out of the lettuce leaves.
4 Divide this mixture between the two leaves.
5 Put the heart of the lettuce on top and roll tightly.
6 You will find that this can be eaten quite easily without knife and fork, and that the introduction

of a new flavour, i.e. horseradish, with fish, is surprisingly good.

To make into a tray meal – serve after vegetable soup, grapefruit or diced melon.

Curried corned beef balls

cooking time: 5–15 minutes

you will need:

1 dessertspoon grated onion	2 oz. breadcrumbs
1 teaspoon curry powder	½ teaspoon Worcestershire sauce
1 oz. fat	6 oz. corned beef
	crisp breadcrumbs

1 Fry the onion and curry powder in melted fat.
2 Add the other ingredients.
3 Form into balls, roll in crisp breadcrumbs.
4 Crisp in the oven or under the grill. Alternatively, they can be fried in hot fat if wished, in which case coat with egg white and crumbs. The yolk of the egg can be mixed with the corned beef. (2 servings)

To make into a tray meal – serve with baked, grilled or fried tomatoes and canned corn on the cob, creamed spinach or asparagus tips.

Cheese and carrot fingers

cooking time: 5 minutes

you will need:

6 oz. grated cheese	pepper
6 oz. grated carrot	mustard
2 oz. butter or margarine	little chopped parsley
good pinch salt	4 slices buttered toast

1 Mix cheese, carrot, butter, salt, pepper, mustard and parsley.
2 Spread on hot buttered toast.
3 Put under fairly hot grill until slightly melted.
4 Cut into fingers.

To make into a tray meal – serve with grilled tomatoes and crisp lettuce.

Cheese boxes

no cooking

you will need:

bread	lettuce
soft cream cheese	tomatoes
cornflakes or chopped nuts	

1 Cut fairly fresh bread into cubes about 1½ inches square.

2 Spread the bread on every side with a soft cream cheese, or grated cheese mixed with a little butter and top of the milk.
3 Roll in crushed cornflakes or chopped nuts.
4 Serve with lettuce and tomatoes.

To make into a tray meal – serve after a cup of soup, choosing one with meat, fish or vegetable flavour, but not one that is topped with cheese.

Midnight sun

cooking time: 10–12 minutes

you will need:

6 rashers streaky bacon	8 oz. grated cheese
4 slices bread	2–3 tablespoons cream
2 oz. margarine	good pinch cayenne pepper
1 teaspoon made mustard	2 tomatoes

1 Cut bacon into 12 half rashers.
2 Cut each of these into 2 strips, making 24 in all.
3 Toast bread, heat margarine and add mustard, cheese, cream and pepper.
4 Spread over toast and brown under grill.
5 Meanwhile, fry bacon and tomatoes (cut into halves) and arrange on top of the cheese to look like rays of sun.

To make into a tray meal – arrange on plates on a bed of crisp lettuce and watercress.

Rice and cheese balls

cooking time: 25 minutes

you will need:

3 oz. rice

for sauce:

1 tablespoon corn oil	1 level teaspoon salt
3 level dessertspoons cornflour	dash cayenne pepper
½ pint milk	1 level teaspoon paprika
3 oz. Parmesan cheese, grated	1 teaspoon onion
½ level teaspoon dry mustard	few drops Worcestershire sauce

to coat:

cornflour	breadcrumbs
1 egg	

to deep fry: corn oil

1 Cook the rice in boiling salted water.
2 Drain very well and leave to cool.
3 Make a sauce with the corn oil, cornflour and milk. *continued*

4 Add the cooked rice and all the other ingredients.

5 Mix well and set aside to chill.

6 Form into small balls.

7 Roll in cornflour and coat twice with egg and breadcrumbs.

8 Fry in corn oil for approximately 1 minute.

9 Serve hot.

To make a tray meal – arrange the cooked balls on hot plates and serve with small cooked cauliflower flowerets and cheese sauce.

Egg and haddock scramble

cooking time: 8 minutes

you will need:

2 oz. margarine	4 eggs
little milk	seasoning
1 small cooked	4 slices bread
Finnan haddock*	

*or part of a larger one

1 Put most of the margarine and about 3 tablespoons milk into a saucepan.

2 Add the flaked fish and heat thoroughly.

3 Stir in the well-seasoned beaten eggs.

4 Cook until the eggs are just set.

5 Toast the slices of bread and spread with the remaining margarine.

6 Top with the fish mixture.

To make into a tray meal – in summer time, this is excellent with a cucumber salad, and in winter serve it with chicory.

Prune kebab

cooking time: 1 hour

you will need:

8–12 prunes*	1–2 dessert apples
4–6 dessertspoons mango chutney	4 oz. processed cheese
4–6 rashers streaky bacon	4 tomatoes, halved and seasoned
8 chipolata sausages	2 oz. melted butter

*well drained canned prunes could be used instead

1 Soak prunes overnight and then simmer until just tender, not over-cooked.

2 Stone prunes and stuff with chutney.

3 Remove bacon rind, wrap each prune in bacon and thread on skewers with sausages, chunks of apple, cheese and tomato.

4 Brush with melted butter.

5 Bake in hot oven (450°F. – Gas Mark 7) for 15 minutes or cook under grill.

6 Serve on skewers with boiled rice.

To make into a tray meal – all that is needed to make a sustaining light meal is to add a crisp salad – a coleslaw (see page 58) to which chopped or grated apple has been added is an excellent flavour combination.

Rice stuffed prunes

cooking time: 1 hour

you will need:

8 oz. prunes*	seasoning
2 oz. cooked rice	paprika pepper
6 oz. cream cheese	

*canned prunes may be used, but drain them very well

1 Soak prunes overnight. Cook until just tender, but not over-cooked.

2 Remove stones.

3 Mix rice and cheese and season well.

4 Fill prunes with this mixture and dust with paprika pepper.

To make into a tray meal – serve with slices of cooked boiled bacon or ham, a little shredded lettuce and crisp buttered toast.

Farmhouse scramble

cooking time: 8 minutes

you will need:

$\frac{1}{2}$ oz. butter or margarine	seasoning
2 eggs	8 oz. cooked mixed vegetables

1 Melt the margarine in a pan and add the well-beaten and seasoned eggs.

2 Cook gently and when half scrambled add the cooked vegetables.

3 Continue cooking until the egg is quite set.

4 Serve on scallop shells or in shallow dishes. (2 servings)

Variations

Cream scramble – add about 3 tablespoons cream to the beaten eggs.

Cheese scramble – add about 2 oz. grated cheese just before the eggs are set – do not over-cook the cheese.

Ham scramble – heat 1–2 oz. chopped cooked ham in 1 oz. butter or margarine. Add the eggs, then the vegetables as in the recipe above.

To make into a tray meal – serve with tomatoes and crisp toast or rolls.

Quick scones with savoury Italian topping

cooking time: 20 minutes

you will need:

for scones:

1 lb. self-raising flour	3 oz. margarine
1 level teaspoon salt	2 medium eggs
2 level teaspoons baking powder	½ pint, less 4 table-spoons, milk

for sauce:

2 tablespoons olive oil	salt and pepper to taste
1 medium onion	½ teaspoon oregano (optional)
1 clove garlic	
4 level tablespoons tomato paste or purée	

for topping:

anchovy fillets, stuffed olives or shrimps, black olives	3 oz. finely grated Cheddar, Cheshire, Gruyère or Mozzarella cheese (if liked use part Parmesan cheese for an extra strong flavour)

1 Make scones. Sift flour, salt and baking powder into bowl.
2 Rub in fat till it resembles fine breadcrumbs.
3 Mix to a soft dough with egg and milk and knead lightly until smooth.
4 If scones are not wanted until later, place dough in a polythene bag and keep in refrigerator or cool larder till ready to bake.
5 Make the sauce by heating the oil, adding onion (finely chopped) and finely chopped garlic.
6 Cook slowly till soft, but not brown.
7 Stir in tomato paste or purée and seasonings and remove from heat.
8 Turn the scone mixture on to a lightly floured board and roll out ½–¾ inch thick.
9 Cut into 8 rounds with a 3-inch cutter and place rounds on greased and floured baking tray, allowing room between each for spreading.
10 Make a 'well' in each round with the base of a jam jar or tumbler about 2½ inches across.
11 Flour base so it will not stick to scones.
12 Fill 'well' with Italian tomato sauce and cover with grated cheese.
13 Top with anchovy fillets and halved stuffed olives or shrimps and black olives.
14 Bake near top of a hot oven (425°F. – Gas Mark 7) for 20 minutes.

Alternative toppings

1 Slices of **salami**, hard-boiled eggs and black olives.
2 Chopped grilled **gammon** and hard-boiled egg.
3 Flaked cooked **fish**, black olives and pimento.
4 **Corned beef** and chopped onion.

To make into a tray meal – this dish is very satisfying, so only needs a crisp green salad as an accompaniment. They can be served cold, but are much nicer hot.

Piperade (with pasta)

cooking time: 12–15 minutes

you will need:

1½ oz. butter	3 eggs
1 small onion, chopped	2 oz. cooked macaroni or noodles – use small shell macaroni, chopped noodles or short cut macaroni
green pepper – if not available use few left over green peas to give colour and little chopped celery or chicory	seasoning
2 skinned tomatoes	slices of buttered toast

1 Heat the butter in the pan and fry the onion, pepper, chopped tomatoes until just soft.
2 Beat the eggs, add the cooked macaroni and season well.
3 Pour into the onion mixture and scramble VERY SLOWLY indeed.
4 Serve on the hot toast.

Variation

Piperade – follow recipe as above, but omit the pasta.

To make into a tray meal – this is a very sustaining egg dish and so forms a complete light meal by itself, ideal if followed by cheese or fresh fruit.

Stuffed mushrooms

cooking time: 10–15 minutes

you will need:

9–12 large mushrooms   little butter or dripping

for filling:

2 onions	seasoning
little butter	3–4 slices bread
2 eggs	parsley

1 Remove stalks, fry mushrooms in hot butter or dripping.
2 Chop mushroom stalks and onions finely. Cook until tender in a very little butter.
3 Add seasoned egg and continue cooking until set.
4 Pile onion filling into mushroom cups, serve on hot toast.
5 Garnish with parsley.

To make into a tray meal – serve with sliced tomatoes or cooked tomatoes, and watercress.

Corned beefburgers

cooking time: 10 minutes

you will need:

1 can corned beef	butter
1 teaspoon mustard	lettuce
2 chopped gherkins or mixed pickles	watercress
	tomatoes
4 large or 8 small rolls	

1 Chop the corned beef and mix with the mustard and chopped gherkins or mixed pickles.
2 Split and butter the rolls, spread with the corned beef mixture. Brush the outside of the rolls with a little butter.
3 Put into a fairly hot oven for about 10 minutes.
4 Meanwhile make a salad of lettuce, watercress and tomatoes, and serve with the beefburgers.

A Meal in a Soup

Providing your soup is a really substantial one, it can be a meal in itself.

The following recipes illustrate the type of soups that can be classed as a supper snack. Any soup becomes more filling and nutritious if topped with grated cheese or chopped hard-boiled eggs. Do not sprinkle on the cheese too early otherwise it will melt and spoil the look of the soup.

Celery broth

cooking time: 1¼–1½ hours

you will need:

6 stalks celery	2 oz. rice
8 oz. minced beef	seasoning
1 onion	parsley
1 oz. margarine or butter	grated cheese
2 pints stock or water and bouillon cube	

1 Chop the stalks of celery into neat pieces.
2 Break the minced beef into small pieces, so no lumps hold together during cooking.
3 Chop the onion finely.
4 Fry in the hot margarine for a few minutes.
5 Add the celery, then the stock and bring to the boil.
6 Put in the beef and stir well for the first 10 minutes.
7 Simmer for about 45 minutes, then add the rice and continue cooking for a further 30–40 minutes.
8 Season well and garnish with chopped parsley and grated cheese.

Variations

Celery chicken broth – use finely chopped chicken instead of meat. If the chicken is cooked then heat for about 5 minutes before adding rice. Use 1½ pints stock only.

Leek broth – use 4 chopped leeks instead of celery.

Dutch broth

cooking time: 40 minutes

you will need:

4 good sized onions	½ pint milk
2 oz. butter	seasoning
1 pint stock or water with bouillon cube	1 egg or egg yolk
	grated cheese
½ oz. cornflour	chopped parsley or watercress

1 Chop the onions and toss until golden brown in the hot butter.
2 Add the stock and simmer for 30 minutes.
3 Blend the cornflour with the milk, add to the onion mixture, bring to the boil and cook until thickened.

4 Add seasoning, then remove from the heat and add the beaten egg or yolk (it could be blended with 1 or 2 tablespoons cream if wished).

5 Cook gently, without boiling, until the egg thickens the liquid.

6 Serve, topped with grated cheese and chopped parsley or watercress.

Variation

Dutch broth gratinée – use recipe as above, but pour the cooked soup into hot soup cups. Top each helping of soup with grated Dutch cheese and brown under the grill or in the oven.

Cheese cream soup

cooking time: 10 minutes

you will need:

2 oz. butter	1 egg (optional)
2 oz. flour	3 tablespoons cream
½ pint chicken stock or water with bouillon cube	6 oz. grated cheese seasoning chopped parsley
½ pint milk	

1 Heat the butter in the pan, stir in the flour and cook for several minutes without browning.

2 Stir in the stock and the milk, bring to the boil and cook until thickened and smooth.

3 Remove from the heat and add the egg, beaten with the cream, cheese and seasoning.

4 Reheat, without boiling, until the cheese is melted, then serve at once. Garnish with the parsley.

Variations

Chicken cheese soup – use recipe for cheese cream soup but add about 4 oz. finely chopped, cooked chicken.

Add this when the sauce has thickened before adding cream etc., and simmer gently for about 5 minutes, then add egg and cream and cheese and continue as before. To allow for the extra cooking, be fairly generous with the ½ pint stock.

Prawn cheese soup – use recipe for cheese cream soup (see above), but add about 4 oz. prawns or shrimps. Substitute water with a little anchovy essence for the chicken stock. Heat the prawns for a few minutes in the sauce before adding egg, cream, etc. To allow for the extra cooking time, use just over the ½ pint milk.

Fish broth

cooking time: 25–30 minutes

you will need:

8 oz. white fish, free from bones and skin	little celery (optional) ¾ pint water or fish stock
1 large onion or 2 smaller ones	

for sauce:

1 oz. butter	seasoning
1 oz. flour	lemon juice
½ pint milk	lemon thyme
little cream or evaporated milk	

1 Cut the raw fish into tiny pieces and chop the onions, and celery if used.

2 To make the fish stock simmer the fish bones and skin in salted water.

3 Cover the fish and onions with the stock and simmer for about 20 minutes until the onion is tender.

4 Make a sauce of the butter, flour and milk, then blend with the fish mixture.

5 Add the cream together with seasoning, including a good squeeze of lemon juice and finely chopped fresh lemon thyme – do not boil when once the lemon juice is added.

Variations:

Golden fish broth – use an extra 1 oz. butter, and fry the diced fish and chopped onion in this until golden brown.

Shellfish broth – use only 4 oz. white fish, then add 4 oz. shelled prawns, shrimps, or chopped lobster meat just before adding the white sauce.

Salmon chowder

cooking time: 25 minutes

you will need:

2 medium onions	seasoning
2 medium potatoes	½ pint milk
2 oz. butter or margarine	8 oz. canned salmon chopped parsley
1 pint water	

1 Peel and dice the onions and potatoes.

2 Toss in the butter until golden coloured.

3 Add the water and seasoning and simmer for 15 minutes until tender.

4 Add the milk and flaked salmon and heat for a further 5 minutes.

5 Garnish with chopped parsley.

Salmon bacon chowder – use recipe for salmon chowder, but use only 1 oz. butter and 2 or 3 rashers diced bacon. Fry the bacon with the butter, then add the onion and potato and cook as before.

Salmon corn chowder – use recipe for salmon chowder, but add about 4 oz. canned or cooked corn with the flaked salmon.

Ham chowder – use recipe for salmon chowder, but add 6 oz. diced cooked ham instead of the salmon.

Shrimp chowder – use recipe for salmon chowder, but use 4–6 oz. shrimps instead of the salmon.

Fish Dishes

Fish is a food that cooks quickly. It is light and easy to digest and therefore an ideal choice for snacks or suppers.

It is not, however, a particularly good food to keep waiting so do not choose fish dishes if you are uncertain of what time the family will be arriving.

As stressed on page 9, when serving fish dishes for television snacks, particular care must be taken to remove sharp bones.

Fish croquettes

cooking time: 20 minutes

you will need:

for sauce:

1 oz. butter or margarine	2 teaspoons capers and/or chopped gherkins
1 oz. flour	4 oz. soft bread-crumbs
¼ pint milk	seasoning
1 lb. cooked white fish	
1 hard-boiled egg	
2 teaspoons chopped parsley	

to coat:

flour	crisp breadcrumbs
1 egg	

to fry:

deep fat or oil

1 Make a thick white sauce with the butter, flour and milk.
2 Add flaked fish, chopped egg and other ingredients.
3 Season well.
4 Form into finger shapes.
5 Coat with flour, egg and crumbs and fry until crisp and golden brown.
6 Serve hot or cold.

Fish rollmops

cooking time: 20 minutes

you will need:

1 teaspoon chopped parsley	seasoning
1 oz. margarine	4 fillets plaice
juice 1 lemon or 2 tablespoons vinegar	water
	pinch mixed spice
	1 onion
	bay leaf

1 Mix the parsley, margarine and a little lemon juice together.
2 Add seasoning.
3 Spread this mixture on to the fillets of fish and roll them up tightly.
4 Put into a dish, adding just enough water to half cover, add remaining lemon juice, seasoning, spice and sliced onion and bay leaf.
5 Put a cover on the dish and cook steadily in the oven for 20 minutes, using a moderate oven (375°F. – Gas Mark 4).
6 Serve hot or cold.

Fish scallops

cooking time: 15 minutes

you will need:

12 oz. flaked cooked fish (salmon, fresh haddock, hake)	seasoning
	1 oz. grated cheese
¼ pint thick white sauce (see page 83)	8 oz. mashed potatoes
	parsley to garnish

1 Stir the fish into the sauce and season thoroughly.
2 Put on to escallop shells and sprinkle over the grated cheese.
3 Carefully pipe round a border of mashed potato.
4 Put under a hot grill for a few minutes until the top is crisp and brown.
5 Garnish with parsley.

Variations

Lobster scallops – flaked canned lobster may be used instead of cooked white fish, or mixed with white fish.

Prawn scallops – whole or chopped prawns may be used instead of white fish, or use half prawns and half white fish.

Fish twists

cooking time: 1 hour

you will need:

4 large fillets plaice, whiting or sole	¼ pint evaporated milk or thin cream
2 large eggs	3 oz. grated cheese
seasoning	lemon
½ pint hot milk	parsley

1 Cut each fillet into two or three thin strips and twist these.
2 Put into a buttered casserole.
3 Beat the eggs with the seasoning, add hot milk, cream and most of the cheese.
4 Pour over the fish twists (straining if necessary).
5 Sprinkle with rest of the cheese and bake in a very moderate oven (300°F. – Gas Mark 3).
6 Garnish with lemon and parsley.

Variation

Salmon royale – use recipe for fish twists, but use approximately 8 oz. cooked flaked fresh or canned salmon at the bottom of the dish.

Savoury fish pie

cooking time: 45 minutes

you will need:

2 onions	1 lb. flaked cooked fish
2 oz. margarine or butter	1 lb. creamed potatoes*
3–4 tomatoes	1 oz. butter

*a short crust pastry topping can be used instead, if preferred

1 Fry thinly sliced onions in margarine.
2 Add 3 or 4 skinned sliced tomatoes and cook until soft.
3 Blend with flaked cooked white fish, season well and put into bottom of a pie dish.

4 Cover with mashed potato and butter and bake for approximately 30 minutes in a moderately hot oven (400°F. – Gas Mark 5).

Variations

Curried fish pie – use recipe for savoury fish pie, but add 1 or 2 teaspoons curry powder to the fried onion and a tablespoon of chutney.

Seafood fish pie – use recipe for savoury fish pie, but add ½–1 teacup shelled shrimps or chopped, shelled prawns and a little anchovy essence.

With pastry – if using pastry, cook in a hot oven (425°F. – Gas Mark 6–7) for 25 minutes.

Fish soufflé pie

cooking time: 40 minutes

you will need:

1 lb. white fish	1 tablespoon capers
milk	1 egg
1 bay leaf	1 oz. grated cheese
2 peppercorns	bacon rolls,
1 tablespoon corn oil	little parsley for
¾ oz. cornflour	garnish
1 tablespoon chopped parsley	

1 Prepare the fish and just cover with milk.
2 Cook with the bay leaf and peppercorns for 7–10 minutes.
3 Strain off the liquid.
4 Remove all skin and bones from the fish and flake it.
5 Make the liquid up to ½ pint with milk, if necessary.
6 Heat the corn oil and add the cornflour.
7 Cook for 1 minute and add the fish liquor.
8 Stir till boiling and boil for 3 minutes stirring all the time.
9 Add the parsley.
10 Use ¼ of the sauce to moisten the fish, add the capers and put this mixture into the bottom of a pie dish.
11 Add the egg yolk and ½ oz. grated cheese to the remaining sauce.
12 Spread this mixture on top of the fish, sprinkle with the remaining ½ oz. cheese.
13 Bake for about 25 minutes in a moderately hot oven (375°F. – Gas Mark 4).
14 Garnish with grilled bacon rolls and parsley.

Hake Portuguese

cooking time: 25–30 minutes

you will need:

4 medium sized hake cutlets	1 large onion
seasoning	3 large tomatoes, skinned
⅛ pint white wine or 1 tablespoon vinegar with 2 tablespoons water	1 oz. breadcrumbs 2 oz. grated cheese 1 oz. butter or margarine

1 Grease dish and put in the fish.
2 Season well and add wine or diluted vinegar.
3 Cover with very thinly sliced onion, thickly sliced tomatoes, breadcrumbs, cheese and butter.
4 Cover with paper and bake in the centre of a moderately hot oven (400°F. – Gas Mark 5).

Herrings with devilled stuffing

cooking time: 10 minutes

you will need:

2 tablespoons breadcrumbs	1–2 tablespoons made mustard
2 tablespoons grated onion	4 herrings
pinch cayenne pepper	2 oz. butter or cooking fat 2 oz. flour

to garnish:

1 lemon	onion

1 Mix together the breadcrumbs, grated onion, cayenne and half the mustard (previously made with a little water).
   If you are not very fond of mustard, cut down on the quantity given.
2 Split and bone the herrings.
3 Spread each fillet with the stuffing and roll up so that the end of the fillet is tucked underneath.
4 Heat the fat or butter in a frying pan and secure each roll with a wooden cocktail stick or short skewer.
5 Turn the rolls in the flour, mixed with the remainder of the dry mustard.
6 When the fat is beginning to smoke, put in the rolls and lower the heat slightly.
7 Fry for 5 minutes on each side.
8 Remove the sticks or skewers and transfer the herring rolls to a serving dish.
9 Garnish with raw or fried onion rings and lemon slices.

Herring and tomato casserole

cooking time: 35 minutes

you will need:

4 medium sized herrings	seasoning knob margarine or butter
4 good sized tomatoes	toast
1 small onion (optional)	

1 Bone, or ask the fishmonger to bone the herrings.
2 Arrange 4 fillets in a wide flat dish.
3 Cover with a layer of sliced tomatoes and the sliced onion.
   Make sure these are very **thinly** sliced.
4 Season.
5 Cover with the rest of the fish and tomatoes.
6 Put a little margarine on top and cook for about 35 minutes in the centre of the oven (400°F. – Gas Mark 5).
7 Serve with crisp toast.

Cheese fish pie

cooking time: 30 minutes

you will need:

1 lb. cooked white fish	½ pint cheese sauce (see page 83)
2 hard-boiled eggs	1 lb. creamed potatoes 3 oz. grated cheese

1 Put flaked cooked white fish and sliced hard-boiled eggs at the bottom of a pie dish.
2 Cover with cheese sauce and creamed potatoes. Sprinkle the grated cheese over the potatoes.
3 Bake for 30 minutes in a moderately hot oven (400°F. – Gas Mark 5).

Variation

Cheese shrimp pie – use recipe above, but use 8–12 oz. shelled shrimps instead of flaked white fish.

Creamed fish pie

cooking time: 30 minutes

you will need:

1 lb. cooked fish	1 lb. creamed potatoes
2 hard-boiled eggs	little butter
½ pint white sauce (see page 83)	

1 Put flaked cooked white fish and sliced hard-boiled eggs at the bottom of a pie dish.

2 Cover with white sauce, creamed potatoes and a little butter.

3 Bake for 30 minutes in a moderately hot oven (400°F. – Gas Mark 5).

Variations

Tuna fish pie – use recipe as above, but use flaked canned tuna instead of cooked fish.

Salmon fish pie – use recipe as before, but use flaked canned salmon instead of cooked fish.

Soused mackerel

cooking time: 1 hour

you will need:

4 large mackerel	½ teaspoon salt
1 small onion	1 teaspoon sweet
1 good teaspoon	spice
pickling spice	¼ pint vinegar
1 teaspoon sugar	2 bay leaves
¼ pint water	1 small sliced apple

1 Split the mackerel, take out backbones, roll them.

2 Put into covered casserole, together with all the other ingredients.

3 Cook in a very moderate oven (300°F. – Gas Mark 2) for 1 hour.

4 Leave until quite cold.

5 Serve with lettuce, potato and beetroot salads.

Variations

Soused herrings – use recipe above, but use herrings instead of mackerel.

Soused white fish – use recipe above, but use 4 cutlets of white fish – hake, cod or halibut.

Jiffy grilled plaice with lemon dressing

cooking time: 9–10 minutes

you will need:

1 oz. margarine or	juice ½ lemon
butter	chopped parsley
seasoning	
1 14-oz. carton frozen	
plaice fillets,	
partially thawed	

1 Melt the margarine in the grill pan.

2 Season the fish and lay it flesh-side down in the pan.

3 Cook for 1 minute, then turn with flesh-side up and grill steadily until golden brown and cooked, about 5–8 minutes, depending on the thickness of fillets.

4 Arrange on a hot serving dish.

5 Add lemon juice to remaining fat in pan, reheat and pour over the fish.

6 Sprinkle with chopped parsley.

Salmon rice loaf with lemon butter

cooking time: 45 minutes

you will need:

1 lb. pink salmon	good pinch celery salt
6 oz. cooked rice	1 grated onion
1 tablespoon	1½ oz. melted butter
parsley	3–4 oz. crushed rice,
1 tablespoon	cereal or crumbs
lemon juice	parsley and lemon to
good pinch salt	garnish
good pinch	
cayenne	

1 Break salmon into small pieces and remove skin and bones.

2 Put into a basin with all other ingredients, except cereal, and mix well.

3 Place in greased loaf pan.

4 Sprinkle with crushed cereal.

5 Bake at 350°F. – Gas Mark 3–4 for 45 minutes. Garnish with parsley and lemon.

6 Serve with lemon butter.

Lemon butter

no cooking

you will need:

2 tablespoons	½ level teaspoon
lemon juice	paprika
3 oz. melted	2 tablespoons chopped
butter	parsley

Mix all ingredients together.

Variations

Use above recipe for Salmon rice loaf, but instead of Lemon butter serve with one of the following butters:

Brown butter or Beurre noir – heat 3 oz. butter until dark brown, add 2 teaspoons vinegar, 2–3 teaspoons chopped parsley and 1–2 teaspoons capers.

Anchovy butter – cream 2–3 oz. butter. Drain the oil from 2–3 anchovy fillets; chop finely, pound well and blend with the butter.

Quick prawn curry

cooking time: 15–20 minutes

you will need:

Patna rice
1 teaspoon curry
  powder
¼ pint mayonnaise
  (see page 57)

8–10 oz. prawns or
  shrimps
about ⅛ pint milk

1 Cook rice in boiling salted water.
2 Meanwhile, blend the curry powder with the mayonnaise.
3 Add the prawns.
4 Put into a pan with milk and heat very gently for 5–10 minutes.
5 Serve on bed of cooked rice.

Cheese and shrimp ramekins

cooking time: 20 minutes

you will need:

4 eggs
½ pint white sauce
  (see page 83)
4 oz. grated
  Cheddar cheese
2–3 oz. shelled
  shrimps

2 teaspoons chopped
  parsley
pinch cayenne pepper
salt
toast to garnish

1 Boil eggs for 7 minutes, then plunge into cold water for 1 minute.
2 Remove shells and roughly chop up the eggs in a small pan with the sauce.
3 Add 2 oz. of the grated cheese, the shrimps and chopped parsley.
4 Heat through without boiling.
5 Season and pour into buttered ramekin dishes.
6 Sprinkle over the remainder of the grated cheese and brown under a hot grill.
7 Garnish and serve at once with crisp toast.

Variation
Cheese and prawn ramekins – use recipe above, but use 2–3 oz. prawns instead of shrimps.

Baked sprats

cooking time: 25–30 minutes

you will need:

sprats
seasoned flour
margarine

lemon wedges
brown bread and
  butter

1 Wash, dry and cut heads from sprats, then coat very lightly with seasoned flour.

2 Arrange in a casserole dish and cover with a little melted margarine.
3 Put on the lid and bake for about 25–30 minutes in a moderate oven (400°F. – Gas Mark 5).
4 Serve with lemon and brown bread and butter.

Haddock pyramids

cooking time: 10–15 minutes
10–15 minutes to boil egg

you will need for 1 serving:

4 oz. cooked
  haddock
1 hard-boiled egg
1 tablespoon
  mayonnaise (see
  page 57)

seasoning
3-4 slices buttered toast
gherkin or olive

1 Mince or flake the fish very finely.
2 Mix with the sieved white of the egg and mayonnaise.
3 Season well and form into a pyramid on the toast.
4 Decorate with a ring of gherkin or olive, and egg yolk.

Variations
Smoked haddock pyramids – use recipe above, but use cooked smoked haddock instead of fresh haddock.
Sardine pyramids – use recipe above, but use canned sardines instead of fresh haddock.
Shrimp pyramids – use recipe above, but use fresh, canned or frozen shrimps instead of haddock.

Left-over Fish

Left-over fish can produce new and interesting quick dishes.

Creamed haddock

Heat a good knob of butter in a pan, add little milk and flaked cooked smoked haddock. Heat together until it forms a thick mixture. If wished, a beaten egg can be stirred into the mixture. Garnish with paprika pepper.

Scrambled kippers

cooking time: 8–10 minutes

you will need:

2 lightly cooked kippers	pepper
4 eggs	2 oz. margarine or butter
2 tablespoons milk	4 slices toast
pinch salt	2 tomatoes

1 Drain and flake the fish coarsely, removing the skin.
2 Beat eggs, add the milk and seasoning (be sparing with the salt) and beat lightly with a fork.
3 Melt 1 oz. of the margarine in a pan, add the eggs and kippers and cook gently, stirring occasionally.
4 Serve on hot toast spread with the remaining margarine.
5 Garnish with tomato rings.

Fish soufflé

cooking time: 35–40 minutes

you will need:

4–6 oz. flaked cooked fish

for sauce:

1 oz. butter or margarine	seasoning
1 oz. plain flour	4 egg whites
¼ pint milk	few drops anchovy essence (optional)
3 egg yolks	

1 Mash fish.
2 Make a thick white sauce with the butter, flour and milk.
3 Add the egg yolks, one at a time, the fish and seasoning.
4 Fold in the stiffly beaten egg whites. Add anchovy essence, if liked.
5 Turn the mixture into a 6-inch buttered soufflé dish (or any other heatproof dish of similar size and shape).
6 Bake in the centre of a moderately hot oven (400°F. – Gas Mark 4).

Variations
Salmon or tuna soufflé – use flaked cooked or canned salmon or tuna fish.
Haddock soufflé – use flaked cooked smoked haddock but be sparing with the salt. A little grated cheese can also be added if liked.

Finnan haddock rarebit

cooking time: 45 minutes

you will need:

1 smoked haddock	1 teaspoon made mustard
1 oz. butter	3–4 oz. grated cheese
1 oz. flour	1–1½ oz. soft bread-crumbs
¼ pint milk	
seasoning	knobs butter for topping
1 tablespoon Worcestershire sauce (light ale can be used)	

1 Cook the haddock and remove the bones and break into large flakes.
2 Put into the casserole.
3 Heat the butter in the pan, stir in the flour and cook for several minutes slowly then add the milk, bring to the boil and cook until thick and smooth.
4 Add seasonings, the sauce or light ale and the cheese, keeping a little back for the topping.
5 Spread over the fish – the mixture is fairly thick, then cover with the crumbs and cheese and knobs of butter.
6 Bake for about 25 minutes in a moderate oven (375°F. – Gas Mark 4).

Variation
Anchovy rarebit – use the above recipe but omit the Worcestershire sauce and the cheese and substitute ½ teaspoon of anchovy essence. Drain the oil off 2 anchovy fillets, chop finely and mix in with the flaked haddock.

Salmon rice soufflé

cooking time: 50 minutes

you will need:

3 eggs	1 8-oz. can pink salmon
seasoning	2 oz. cooked long grain rice
1 oz. margarine	
1 oz. flour	
¼ pint milk	

1 Separate the egg yolks from the whites.
2 Make a sauce of the margarine, flour and milk.
3 Add can of salmon, the rice and stir in the egg yolks and seasoning.
4 Add the stiffly beaten egg whites.
5 Put into prepared soufflé dish and bake for approximately 30 minutes in the centre of a moderate oven (375°F. – Gas Mark 4).

Salmon rice croquettes

cooking time: 30–35 minutes

you will need:

2 tablespoons rice
5 tablespoons water
1 medium sized
  can salmon
pepper and salt
2 teaspoons lemon
  juice

1 egg
2–3 tablespoons
  breadcrumbs
watercress
lemon slices

1 Add rice to boiling salted water, stir well.
2 Cover saucepan, allow to come to the boil.
3 Reduce heat and cook until rice is tender – about 15 minutes.
4 Flake salmon with a fork.
5 Add pepper and salt, rice and lemon juice.
6 Blend well together.
7 Form into croquettes and allow to stand for 15 minutes to settle firmly into shape.
8 Brush with egg and roll in breadcrumbs.
9 Place in buttered ovenware dish and bake for 15–20 minutes in a very moderate oven (350°F. – Gas Mark 3).
10 Serve with watercress and lemon slices.
  For the unexpected guest – accompany with canned asparagus tips, frozen or canned peas, and crisp fingers of toast.

Meat, Canned Meat and Sausage Dishes

While many meat dishes are considered too substantial for a snack, there are others which can provide an attractive meal within a very short time, without being too filling. Some of the recipes on the following pages are easy and interesting ways to use up those small portions of meat that have been left over from the main meal.

Only reheat cooked meat or it becomes tough and tasteless.

Savoury horns

no cooking

you will need:

2 oz. cream cheese
2 dessertspoons
  tomato sauce
little horseradish
  cream (optional)
few olives or gherkins
  or beetroot, sliced

seasoning
6 thin lean slices
  cooked meat
lettuce
tomatoes

1 Beat the cream cheese until light.
2 Add the tomato sauce, horseradish cream and the slices of olives. Season well.
3 Spread each slice of meat with this mixture and roll into horns.
4 Serve on a bed of lettuce and garnish with olives and tomato roses.

Quick beef olives

cooking time: 40–45 minutes

you will need:

packet of stuffing
4 thin slices
  topside of beef

1 can of tomato or
  mushroom or mixed
  vegetable soup

1 Make the stuffing.
2 Put it on each slice of beef and roll firmly.
3 Put into a casserole and pour over the slightly diluted soup.
4 Cook for 45 minutes in the centre of a moderate oven (375°F. – Gas Mark 4).

Variation

Gammon olives – use recipe above, but use 4 thin slices of gammon instead of beef.

Veal cutlets

cooking time: 30–35 minutes

you will need:

4 veal cutlets
egg and bread-
  crumbs
2 tablespoons
  corn oil
½ pint mushroom
  sauce* (see page
  83)

4 tablespoons sour
  cream
lemon slices
parsley

*or mushroom soup or ready prepared sauce

1 Trim the cutlets and coat twice in egg and breadcrumbs.
2 Heat the corn oil and oven fry the cutlets for 25–30 minutes in a moderate oven (375°F. – Gas Mark 4).
3 Baste occasionally.
4 Make the mushroom sauce.
5 Add the sour cream.
6 Pour around the cutlets.
7 Garnish with lemon slices and parsley.

Jambalaya

cooking time: 25 minutes

you will need:

2 tablespoons olive oil
1 medium sized onion
2 sticks celery or canned celery or chicory
8 oz. cooked long grain rice
8 oz. canned peeled tomatoes
8 oz. frankfurter sausages or cooked meat
salt and pepper to taste
1 tablespoon chopped parsley
grated Parmesan cheese

1 Heat the oil in a frying pan and cook the chopped onion and celery over gentle heat until soft and golden.
2 Add the rice and stir until thoroughly mixed.
3 Add the tomatoes, sausages, seasoning and parsley.
4 Cook and heat gently.
5 Serve very hot and serve Parmesan cheese separately.

Sausages and barbecue sauce

cooking time: 15–35 minutes

you will need:

1½ lb. sausages
barbecue sauce

1 Fry or grill or bake the sausages in the oven until golden brown.
2 Keep hot and serve with barbecue sauce.

Barbecue sauce

cooking time: 20–25 minutes

you will need:

1 large onion
2 oz. fat
1 oz. flour
1 teaspoon curry powder
½ pint water or stock
1 lb. tomatoes, skinned
½ teaspoon chilli sauce
½ teaspoon Worcestershire sauce
seasoning
pinch sugar

1 Chop the onion into small pieces and fry in the fat until tender but not brown.
2 Add the flour and curry powder and cook for several minutes.

3 Add the water or stock with the chopped tomatoes (skinned if possible).
4 Bring to the boil and cook until smooth.
5 Add the sauces and seasoning together with the sugar.
6 Sieve if wished.

Bacon and beef fritters

cooking time: 8 minutes

you will need:

12 oz. finely diced, cooked beef
4 oz. finely diced, cooked ham
6 oz. self raising flour
pinch salt
pinch celery salt
2 eggs
12 tablespoons milk

to fry:

fat or oil

1 Mix beef and ham together. Make a thick batter with flour, seasonings, eggs and milk.
2 Add meat mixture. Drop spoonfuls into hot shallow or deep fat, or oil. Cook until golden.
3 Drain. Serve with a green salad.

Bacon TV snacks

cooking time: 15 minutes

you will need:

12 rashers back bacon, cut thinly
4 small frankfurter sausages
4 fingers cheese
2 lamb's kidneys
2 bananas
watercress

1 Cut the rind off the bacon.
2 Split the sausages and insert fingers of cheese.
3 Roll 4 rashers bacon round these and secure with cocktail sticks.
4 Halve kidneys, season and roll 4 more rashers bacon round these, securing again with cocktail sticks.
5 Wrap the bacon round halved bananas and secure.
6 Grill or pop into a hot oven (450°F. – Gas Mark 6).
7 Serve with watercress.

Ham loaf de luxe

cooking time: 35 minutes

you will need:

about 10 oz. cooked ham	1 egg to bind
2 teaspoons grated onion or chopped chives	1 tablespoon cream or top of milk
2 teaspoons parsley	seasoning
I can corn or corn with peppers	2 hard-boiled eggs

1 Mince the ham and mix with the onion, parsley, drained corn or corn and peppers and the egg and cream.
2 Season lightly and press into a greased loaf tin.
3 Use half the mixture, then arrange the 2 shelled eggs on top of this.
4 Cover with rest of mixture.
5 Put a piece of foil or greased greaseproof paper over the mixture and bake in the centre of a moderate oven (375°F. – Gas Mark 4).
6 Turn out and serve hot.

Devilled chicken

cooking time: 12 minutes

you will need:

12 oz. cold cooked chicken	¼ teaspoon black pepper
2 teaspoons tomato ketchup	2 teaspoons made mustard
2 teaspoons vinegar	2 tablespoons olive oil
pinch cayenne pepper	

1 Cut the chicken into neat pieces.
2 Blend all the other ingredients together.
3 Brush this over the chicken and grill until browned on both sides.
4 Serve cold with salad or hot with boiled rice, vegetables and sweet chutney.

Chicken livers Diane

cooking time: 8 minutes

you will need:

2 large rashers bacon	2 slices bread
4 chicken livers	Worcestershire sauce
seasoning	little butter
	watercress garnish

1 Halve rashers of bacon, wrap round livers which should be well seasoned.
2 Put on to skewers and cook **steadily** under grill.
3 Toast the bread.

4 Blend 2 or 3 drops sauce with a little butter and spread over toast.
5 Top with the bacon and liver rolls and watercress. This recipe makes 4 light or 2 substantial snacks.

Chicken quenelles

cooking time: 20 minutes

you will need for 3 good servings:

8 oz. cooked chicken	2 good tablespoons soft breadcrumbs
1 oz. butter or margarine	2 rashers bacon
1 oz. flour	crisp breadcrumbs
¼ pint milk or chicken stock	fat for frying
seasoning	parsley
1 egg	tomatoes

1 Put the cooked chicken through a mincer.
2 Heat the margarine or butter in a pan, stir in the flour and cook for several minutes.
3 Take the pan off the heat and gradually add the cold milk.
4 Bring to the boil, stirring all the time.
5 Continue cooking until a really thick sauce and add seasoning. Leave to cool.
6 When the sauce is cold, stir in the chicken, half the egg and breadcrumbs.
7 Form into 6 small shapes, rather like sausages.
8 Divide each rasher of bacon into 3 pieces and wrap 1 piece of bacon round each quenelle.
9 Dip in the rest of the egg and coat thoroughly in crisp breadcrumbs.
10 Heat the fat in a pan and fry the quenelles until crisp and brown.
11 Continue cooking slowly for few minutes.
12 Decorate with parsley and fried or grilled tomatoes.

Turkey Creole

cooking time: 20 minutes

you will need:

4 oz. long grain rice	¼ pint turkey stock
1 oz. fat	about 12 oz. sliced cooked turkey meat
1 green pepper	seasoning
1 head celery (or 1 can celery)	3 large tomatoes

1 Cook rice in boiling salted water.
2 Heat fat and toss in sliced pepper and large pieces celery.
3 Add stock.

4 Simmer until vegetables are nearly cooked.
5 Add turkey and season well.
6 When thoroughly hot, arrange on bed of cooked rice.
7 Garnish with sliced tomato.

Variation

Chicken Creole – use the above recipe, but substitute 12 oz. sliced cooked chicken for the turkey meat and substitute chicken stock for the turkey stock.

Turkey à la king

cooking time: 15 minutes

you will need:

1 sliced red pepper	12 oz. diced cooked turkey
2 oz. mushrooms	
2 oz. butter	1 tablespoon sliced olives
½ pint white sauce (made partly with turkey stock) (see page 83)	seasoning
	4 slices toast
	olives garnish

1 Fry pepper and mushrooms in butter or cook under grill until soft.
2 Stir into sauce. Add other ingredients and mix well.
3 Pile on to toast.
4 Garnish with olives.

Bacon and sausage puffs

cooking time: 15 minutes

you will need:

4 rashers long streaky bacon (or bacon pieces)	8 oz. sausage meat

for batter:

2 oz. flour	fat for frying
seasoning	4 tomatoes
1 egg	
just over ⅛ pint milk and water	

1 Chop the bacon finely and mix with the sausage meat.
2 Form into 8 small or 4 large rounds.
3 Make the batter by mixing the flour with a pinch of salt, adding egg and milk to give smooth thick batter.
4 Coat the sausage mixture with this and cook in fat until crisp and golden brown.
5 Drain and serve with fried tomatoes.

Variation

Ham and sausage puffs – make above recipe but use 4 oz. finely chopped cooked ham for the bacon rashers.

Bacon beignets

cooking time: 1 hour for bacon, 5 minutes to fry

you will need:

1 lb. bacon (forehock, collar or gammon)	1 teaspoon basil or marjoram
	2 eggs
8 oz. plain flour	¼ pint milk
seasoning	⅛ pint beer or water

to fry:

deep lard

1 Cook bacon by simmering gently.
2 Sieve the flour, seasoning and herbs into a bowl and add the eggs.
3 Gradually mix in the milk, then the beer or water.
4 Beat well and allow to stand for at least 1 hour.
5 Cut the bacon into 1-inch cubes and dip each piece into the batter.
6 Fry in deep lard until golden brown.
7 Drain on crumpled kitchen paper and serve with red cabbage or green vegetable and a savoury sauce (see pages 83 and 84).

Savoury ham and potatoes au gratin

cooking time: 35 minutes

you will need:

4 tablespoons corn oil	2 tablespoons sweet red pepper (capsicum), chopped
1 lb. potatoes, parboiled and sliced	4 oz. cheese, grated
	salt and pepper
8 oz. cooked ham, diced	¾ pint onion sauce* (see page 83)

*or sauce mix or cream of onion soup.

1 Heat the corn oil and sauté the potatoes until lightly browned.
2 Arrange the potatoes (keeping a few for the top), ham, red pepper and 3½ oz. of the cheese in layers in a casserole.
3 Season with salt and pepper.
4 Make the onion sauce.
5 Pour over the ingredients in the casserole.
6 Bake for 20 minutes in a moderate oven (375°F. – Gas Mark 4).
7 When cooked, place the remaining slices of potatoes on top.
8 Sprinkle with cheese and brown under the grill.

Ham and macaroni casserole

cooking time: 15–30 minutes

you will need:

4 oz. chopped ham
4 hard-boiled eggs
2 oz. cooked
   macaroni

½ pint cheese sauce
   (see page 83)
few breadcrumbs
2 oz. grated cheese

1 Mix the chopped ham, eggs and macaroni with the cheese sauce.
2 Put into a shallow buttered dish.
3 Top with crumbs and cheese and brown under grill or in the oven.

Variations

Ham and potato casserole – use about 4 cooked potatoes instead of macaroni.

Ham and leek casserole – use 4 cooked leeks instead of macaroni.

Potted meat

If you have a refrigerator, a home-made potted meat is very good to store. Use slices for sandwich fillings, serve it as fingers with salad and it is very good spread over slices of hot buttered toast, covered with grated cheese and then browned under the grill.

cooking time: 2 hours

you will need:

6 pig's trotters
good pinch mixed
   herbs*
small bunch parsley

2 bay leaves
1½ lb. flank beef or
   cheap stewing beef
seasoning

*for extra flavour add more herbs, onions, etc.

1 Wash pig's trotters.
2 Put into a saucepan with the herbs, etc.
3 Add strips of meat and simmer gently in water to cover for approximately 2 hours or until the meat feels quite tender.
4 Put the meat through a coarse mincer. You may like to do it twice or mince it more finely.
5 Remove the meat from the trotters and put this through the mincer at the same time.
6 Put the meat into a basin and then boil the stock hard in a saucepan until this is reduced to approximately ½ pint.
7 Strain over the meat and allow to set.

Supper snacks using canned meat

There is a large range of canned meats on the market – luncheon meat, chopped pork meat, corned beef, etc. – and the following recipes are suitable for any of these.

While a specific type of canned meat has been used in every recipe, this can, of course, be varied by using the different kinds of meat available.

Fritters of corned beef

1 Cut meat into fairly thick slices.
2 Stir a little grated onion, chopped parsley and seasoning into a thick batter (see page 12).
3 Dip slices of meat in this and fry in hot fat until golden brown.
4 Serve with fried tomatoes.

Fricassée of luncheon meat

1 Make a well flavoured white sauce (see page 83) adding a little grated cheese if liked and a rasher of grilled chopped bacon.
2 Heat squares of diced luncheon meat in the sauce.
3 Serve on a bed of well drained rice.

Curried corned beef

Serve diced meat in a good curry sauce (see page 13).

Stuffed tomatoes

1 Choose large firm tomatoes.
2 Remove centre, chop finely, then mix with a little chopped chives or onion, finely diced meat and seasoning.
3 Return to tomato cases with knob of butter or margarine on top.
4 Bake for 15–20 minutes in hot oven (450°F. – Gas Mark 6).

Potato meat cakes

cooking time: 10–12 minutes

you will need:

1 large can luncheon meat	1 egg
8 oz. mashed potato	crisp breadcrumbs
	fat for frying

1 Mash the luncheon meat and mix with the potato.
2 Separate the egg yolk from the white.
3 Add yolk of egg to the luncheon meat mixture.
4 Form into round cakes.
5 Brush with the slightly whisked egg white and roll in the crumbs.
6 Fry until crisp and golden brown.
7 Serve with salad.

Variation

Potato meat hash – use ingredients as before, but add beaten egg to potato and luncheon meat, season well. No breadcrumbs are required. Heat fat in pan and put in the mixture, fry steadily until golden brown.
Fold and serve like an omelette, garnish with chopped parsley and serve with red cabbage or chutney.

Fried pork and ham with mushrooms

cooking time: 15 minutes

you will need:

1 medium sized can chopped pork and ham	1 tablespoon cornflour
little fat for frying	little milk
mushroom sauce (see page 83) or	1 oz. margarine or butter
1 can condensed mushroom soup	fried bacon rashers (optional)

1 Cut the chopped pork and ham into fairly thick slices and fry in hot fat.
2 Prepare mushroom sauce – a can of condensed mushroom soup can be used.
3 Blend cornflour with little cold milk.
4 Stir into mushroom mixture, together with butter or margarine.
5 Heat steadily stirring all the time until a thickened sauce.
6 Arrange the meat on a hot dish and coat with the sauce.
7 Top with rashers of fried bacon if wished.

Pork toasties

cooking time: 8 minutes

you will need:

1 large can pork luncheon meat	little mustard
toast	little butter

1 Cut luncheon meat into slices.
2 Cover pieces of hot buttered toast with a little mustard then the luncheon meat.
3 Brush with butter.
4 Grill steadily, turning the meat once, so both sides are hot and golden brown.
5 Serve with pickles – chutney, salad or grilled tomatoes.

Fried 'steaks' of pork

Cut luncheon meat into fairly thick slices. Fry steadily in a little hot fat.
Serve with fried tomatoes and vegetables.

Variation

Cheese pork toasties – use recipe above, but put a slice of cheese under the luncheon meat, or cover the grilled luncheon meat with cheese and return to the grill to toast this.

Savoury fritters

cooking time: 8 minutes

you will need:
for the batter:

4 oz. self-raising flour (with plain flour 1 teaspoon baking powder)	$\frac{1}{4}$ pint milk or milk and water
seasoning	1 large can luncheon meat
1 egg	fat for deep frying

1 Sieve the flour and seasoning together.
2 Add the egg and milk gradually to give a smooth thick batter.
3 Cut the luncheon meat into neat slices.
4 Coat with the batter.
5 Fry in hot fat until crisp and golden brown. (Deep fat is best for this recipe.)

Five-minute casserole

cooking time: 5 minutes

you will need:

1 large can luncheon meat	little milk or water
1 large can tomato or vegetable soup	toast or vegetables

1 Cut the luncheon meat into slices, fingers or neat dice.
2 Pour the soup into a pan and dilute with a very little water or milk if too thick.
3 Add the meat and heat for about 5 minutes.
4 Serve with crisp toast or vegetables.

Pork mixed grill

cooking time: 8 minutes

you will need:

1 large can pork luncheon meat	mushrooms
tomatoes	little butter or margarine
rashers bacon	

1 Cut luncheon meat into slices.
2 Put these on the grid of a grill pan with halved tomatoes, rashers of bacon and mushrooms.
3 Brush lightly with the fat.
4 Cook until hot and golden.
5 Serve with vegetables or a crisp salad.

Pork and ham Florentine

cooking time: 25 minutes

you will need:

frozen or fresh spinach	1 medium sized can chopped pork and ham
butter	
seasoning	6 eggs
6 slices bread	

1 Cook the spinach.
2 Drain and chop.
3 Heat with a little butter and seasoning.
4 Toast the bread.
5 Cover the slices with chopped pork and ham and a little butter.
6 Heat under the grill.
7 Fry or poach the eggs.
8 When meat is golden coloured top with spinach and egg.

Pork and ham au gratin

cooking time: 25–30 minutes

you will need:

1 medium sized can chopped pork and ham	2 oz. grated cheese
	few breadcrumbs
¼ pint cheese sauce (see page 83)	little butter

1 Cut the chopped pork and ham into slices and arrange in a shallow dish.
2 Cover with the cheese sauce, grated cheese, breadcrumbs and a little butter.
3 Cook for approximately 25 minutes in a moderately hot oven (400°F. – Gas Mark 5) until the top is crisp and golden brown.

Savoury risotto

cooking time: 15 minutes

you will need:

2 oz. margarine	seasoning
3 tomatoes	1 medium size can corned beef or luncheon meat
1 onion, thinly sliced	
3 oz. boiled, well drained rice	little milk
	2 oz. grated cheese

1 Heat the margarine, then fry sliced tomatoes and onion until just soft.
2 Add rice, seasoning, diced luncheon or corned meat and little milk.
3 Heat thoroughly, then lastly stir in the cheese.

Corned beef cutlets

cooking time: 15–20 minutes

you will need:

for sauce:

1 oz. margarine	1 12-oz. can corned beef
1 oz. flour	
¼ pint milk or stock	seasoning
1 breakfast cup breadcrumbs	

to coat:

1 egg	fat
crisp breadcrumbs	

1 Make the sauce by heating the margarine in the pan, stirring in the flour and cooking for 2 minutes, then adding the liquid.
2 Bring to the boil and cook until thick.
3 Add the breadcrumbs and the flaked corned beef.
4 Season well.

5 Form into cutlet shapes.

6 Coat with beaten egg and crisp breadcrumbs and fry in hot fat until crisp and golden brown.

7 Serve hot with fried tomatoes, peas and sauté potatoes, or serve cold with salad.

Corned beef fritters

cooking time: 8 minutes

you will need:	for batter:
6 oz. corned beef	2 oz. plain flour
1 teaspoon chopped parsley	1 egg yolk
pinch mixed herbs	⅛ pint milk
seasoning	
1 oz. dripping or cooking fat for frying	

1 Mix the flour, egg and milk into a thick batter.

2 Flake the corned beef and add this to the batter, together with the other ingredients.

3 Melt the fat in a frying pan and when really hot drop in spoonfuls of the batter mixture.

4 Fry quickly until crisp and brown on both sides.

5 Serve as soon as possible after they are cooked.

Pork toad-in-the-hole

cooking time: 35–40 minutes

you will need:

for batter:	
4 oz. flour	1 medium size can luncheon meat
salt	
1 egg	1 oz. fat
½ pint milk or milk and water	

1 Sieve the flour and salt together.

2 Add the egg and gradually beat in the milk to give a smooth thin batter.

3 Cut the luncheon meat into thick slices and then into fingers.

4 Arrange these with the fat at the bottom of a Yorkshire pudding tin or heat-resisting dish.

5 Put into a hot oven (425–450°F. – Gas Mark 6–7) for about 10 minutes.

6 Pour over the batter and cook for a further 25–30 minutes, lowering the heat slightly if necessary towards the end of the cooking time.

7 Serve at once with vegetables.

Variation

Harlequin toad-in-the-hole – use method as for pork toad-in-the-hole, but also heat halved tomatoes, mushrooms with the luncheon meat.

Corned beef hash

cooking time: 15 minutes

you will need:	
½ oz. dripping	8 oz. cooked potatoes, sliced
2 onions	
8 oz. corned beef	8 oz. tomatoes
	seasoning

1 Melt the fat in the frying pan and fry the grated onions for 2 or 3 minutes.

2 Add the corned beef, potatoes, and the sliced tomatoes. Season well.

3 Cook slowly until brown on the underside.

4 Fold over like an omelette and serve.

Variations

With mashed potato – use ingredients as above, but mash the potatoes and flake the meat, blend together with the fried grated onion and seasoning.

With tomatoes – the tomatoes can be skinned and chopped and mixed with the potatoes, etc., or they can be omitted from the hash and fried separately. Serve with red cabbage.

Pork and ham scramble

cooking time: 12 minutes

you will need:	
1 12-oz. can chopped pork and ham	seasoning
	2 tablespoons milk
1½ oz. butter	toast
4–5 eggs	parsley
	chives

1 Cut the meat into neat cubes.

2 Put into a saucepan with the butter and heat for a few minutes.

3 Beat and season eggs, adding about 2 tablespoons milk.

4 Pour over the meat and allow to cook very slowly.

5 Pile on to hot buttered toast.

6 Garnish with chopped parsley and chives.

Pork and ham soufflé rarebit

cooking time: 15 minutes

you will need:

4–6 slices bread	2 eggs
1 medium sized	4 oz. grated cheese
can chopped	1 oz. butter
pork and ham	seasoning
butter for brushing	

1 Toast the bread.
2 Cover with the sliced pork and ham.
3 Brush with butter and heat gently for a few minutes under the grill.
4 Meanwhile prepare the rarebit mixture, by separating the egg yolks from the whites.
5 Blend the yolks with the cheese, the butter and seasoning.
6 Fold in stiffly beaten egg whites.
7 Spread carefully over the meat and return to the grill until golden brown, or heat in a moderately hot oven for 10 minutes.

Luncheon meat salads

Pork and apple salad

1 Slice luncheon meat thinly and arrange on a bed of crisp lettuce.
2 Garnish with rings of dessert apple topped with mayonnaise and sliced tomatoes.

Onion and beetroot salad

1 Slice luncheon meat thinly and arrange on bed of lettuce with rings of raw onion and chopped pickled beetroot.
2 Garnish with pickled capers.

Stuffed tomato salad

1 Cut off the tops of large firm tomatoes.
2 Scoop out the centre pulp.
3 Chop and season this and mix with diced pork luncheon meat, binding with a little mayonnaise if wished.
4 Pile back into tomato cases.
5 Garnish with sliced hard-boiled eggs and lettuce.

Quick supper snacks using canned frankfurters or cocktail sausages

It is extremely useful to keep one or two cans of these sausages in the cupboard, for while they can be eaten cold they are equally good as a hot dish. You can buy frankfurter sausages in your delicatessen shop and they keep for several days in a cold place.

Stuffed jacket potatoes

cooking time: 1½ hours

you will need:

4 good sized	1 can frankfurter
potatoes	sausages or cocktail
little butter or	sausages
margarine	3 tomatoes
seasoning	little fried onion
	little bacon, if wished

1 Bake the potatoes in the oven until soft.
2 Cut off a slice from the tops.
3 Remove centre pulp and mash with a little butter or margarine and seasoning.
4 Drain and slice sausages and mix with the skinned, chopped tomatoes, seasoning and onion and/or bacon.
5 Put this mixture into the potato cases.
6 Top with mashed potato and return to a moderately hot oven (400°F. – Gas Mark 5) for about 25 minutes when the filling is hot and the potato crisped on top.

Frankfurter in brine

As these particular sausages are in liquid, they can be served in the continental way, i.e. heating so that they retain their moisture.

Sauerkraut and sausages

1 Heat the sauerkraut and toss in a little butter or margarine.
2 Arrange on a hot dish.
3 Heat the sausages in the brine as directed on the can.
4 Drain and arrange round the sauerkraut.

Frankfurter pin wheel

cooking time: 15–20 minutes

you will need:

for sauce:

1 oz. butter or	2 large carrots
margarine	1 cooked pastry case
1 oz. flour	1 medium sized can
⅜ pint milk	frankfurter sausages
4 oz. grated cheese	2 oz. cheese
seasoning	

1 Make a thick roux sauce with the butter, flour, milk and 4 oz. of the cheese, seasoning well.

2 Add the coarsely grated raw carrots to the sauce.

3 Spread the mixture into the pastry case.

4 Arrange the sausages on top in the shape of spokes of a wheel.

5 Cover with the rest of the cheese.

6 Heat in a hot oven (425°F. – Gas Mark 6) for 10 minutes.

7 Serve hot or cold.

Frankfurter and tomato bake

cooking time: 30 minutes

you will need:

1 medium sized can frankfurter sausages	½ pint tomato sauce (see page 84) or tomato soup

1 Drain the sausages and put into a dish.

2 Cover with tomato sauce or tomato soup.

3 Heat in a moderate oven (375°F. – Gas Mark 4).

4 Serve with creamed spinach.

Macaroni special

cooking time: 10–25 minutes

you will need:

3 oz. cooked macaroni	1 small sized can frankfurter sausages or 4–8 sausages
¾ pint cheese sauce (see page 83)	2 tomatoes
	2 oz. grated cheese

1 Mix the macaroni with the cheese sauce and put into a heat-resistant dish.

2 Arrange the sausages and sliced tomato on top.

3 Cover with grated cheese.

4 Heat through under the grill, or in oven.

Apple rings and sausages

cooking time: 12 minutes

you will need:

cooking apples butter or bacon fat	1 medium sized can sausages in brine

1 Peel, core and slice large cooking apples.

2 Fry until just tender in butter or bacon fat.

3 Meanwhile heat sausages in brine as directed on the can.

4 Drain and insert through the centre of each cooked apple ring.

Cheese frankfurters

cooking time: 10–15 minutes

you will need:

8 frankfurter sausages	4 rashers bacon
4 oz. Cheddar or processed cheese	

1 Slit each sausage and cut cheese into 8 strips. Insert a strip in the centre of each sausage.

2 Halve rashers of bacon and wrap round the sausages, secure with wooden cocktail sticks.

3 Put into a dish and bake in a moderately hot oven until bacon is crisp.

Cocktail sausages in beer

cooking time: 35 minutes

you will need:

potatoes	½ pint brown ale
1 medium sized can sausages in brine	1 tablespoon flour
	1 carrot, sliced
	1 onion, sliced

1 Cook and cream potatoes and arrange in a border on a hot dish.

2 Heat the sausages in their brine as directed on the can.

3 Lift out of the brine and arrange in the centre of potato border.

4 Add the brown ale to the brine blended with the flour.

5 Heat until thickened slightly.

6 Pour some over the sausages and serve the rest separately.

7 Garnish with sliced carrot and fried onion rings.

Tomato sausages

cooking time: 8–10 minutes

you will need:

1 medium sized can cocktail sausages	1 tablespoon concentrated tomato purée **or** 2–3 tablespoons tomato ketchup **or** 2 or 3 tomatoes

1 Pour the brine from the can of sausages into a saucepan together with the tomato purée, tomato ketchup or skinned and chopped tomatoes.

2 Heat gently until tomato and brine mixture is smooth and boiling.

3 Put in the sausages and let them stand in the hot liquid without boiling, until heated through.

Egg Dishes

The variety of dishes that can be made from eggs is almost unbelievable and they are, of course, the ideal ingredient for a snack when you are short of time.

Generally speaking, it is better to wait until the family are ready before you cook egg dishes, for they can so easily be spoilt and since the cooking is usually only a matter of minutes, there is no point in getting them ready too soon.

Savoury eggs

no cooking

you will need:

4 hard-boiled eggs	stuffed olives
cooked meat or fish	aspic jelly
tomato sauce	lettuce or other salad
seasoning	vegetables

1 Cut the eggs in halves lengthways.
2 Remove yolks and mix with cooked meat, tomato sauce and seasoning.
3 Pile back into the egg-white shells.
4 Garnish with stuffed olives and serve on a dish surrounded with small mounds of aspic jelly and lettuce, or other salad vegetables.

Savoury egg flan

no cooking

you will need:

1 beef bouillon cube	1 pastry flan case,
½ pint water	cooked
½ oz. gelatine,	3 hard-boiled eggs
(powdered)	3 tomatoes
squeeze lemon juice	lettuce

1 Dissolve beef cube in ¼ pint hot water.
2 Add gelatine and when completely dissolved add lemon juice and ¼ pint cold water.
3 Leave in a cool place.
4 Fill flan case with hard-boiled shelled and quartered eggs and skinned and quartered tomatoes.
5 When gelatine is just setting, spoon mixture over the eggs and tomatoes, filling the flan.
6 Allow any surplus aspic to set.
7 Served chopped with the flan on a lettuce bed.

Anchovy eggs

no cooking

you will need:

4 hard-boiled eggs	1 teaspoon essence of
1 tablespoon salad	anchovies
cream	capers
	salad

1 Cut the eggs in half.
2 Remove yolks carefully, sieve and mix with salad cream and anchovy essence.
3 Pipe or pile this mixture into the egg-white shells.
4 Garnish with capers and salad.

Egg coleslaw

no cooking

you will need:

3 hard-boiled eggs	3 dessertspoons
1 small white	salad cream
cabbage	paprika pepper

1 Chop 2 of the eggs, mix with shredded cabbage and salad cream.
2 Put in a shallow dish and garnish with the third egg sliced, and paprika pepper.

Swiss eggs

cooking time: 10 minutes

you will need:

butter	1 oz. grated cheese
4 oz. Gruyère	4 eggs
cheese, sliced	seasoning
	parsley

1 Butter a shallow dish or 4 individual dishes and cover the bottom of the dish or dishes with thinly sliced cheese.
2 Break the eggs carefully on to the cheese slices, season and cover with the rest of the cheese which should be finely grated.
3 Bake for approximately 10 minutes in a moderately hot oven until the eggs are lightly set.
4 Garnish with parsley.

Variation

With cream – a little butter can be put on top

with the cheese and a small quantity of cream poured over the eggs before covering with grated cheese.

Salad eggs

no cooking

you will need:

2 hard-boiled eggs	3 tablespoons salad
2 oz. cooked ham	cream
2 gherkins	salad vegetables

1 Cut eggs in half lengthwise.
2 Remove yolks and chop.
3 Mix chopped ham and gherkins together and place a spoonful into egg-white shells.
4 Cover with salad cream, sprinkle yolk on top, and garnish with salad vegetables.

Sardine eggs

no cooking

you will need:

4 hard-boiled eggs	1 teaspoon anchovy
4 boned sardines	essence
2 tablespoons thick	1 dessertspoon pickled
white sauce (see	gherkins, finely
page 83) or	chopped
mayonnaise	watercress

1 Cut eggs in half lengthwise.
2 Remove yolks from the halved hard-boiled eggs and pound with the other ingredients.
3 Replace in egg-white shells.
4 Serve with watercress.

Hard-boiled egg cutlets

cooking time: 10 minutes

you will need for 2 servings:

1 oz. margarine or	2 hard-boiled eggs
butter	4 tablespoons
1 oz. flour	breadcrumbs
¼ pint milk	seasoning
seasoning	crisp breadcrumbs for
	coating
	fat for frying

1 Make white sauce. Heat margarine in a saucepan.

2 Stir in flour and cook for several minutes.
3 Take pan off the heat and add cold milk. Add seasoning.
4 Return to heat and bring slowly to the boil.
5 Continue boiling until thick and smooth.
6 Add chopped hard-boiled eggs and breadcrumbs.
7 Let mixture cool, taste and re-season if necessary.
8 Form into cutlet shapes, brush with a little milk and toss in crisp breadcrumbs.
9 Fry until crisp and brown.
10 Drain well.

Egg and tomato cutlets

cooking time: 15 minutes

you will need for 2 servings:

1 oz. margarine	2 tablespoons
1 oz. flour	breadcrumbs
¼ pint tomato	seasoning
juice or thin	little milk
purée	crisp breadcrumbs for
1 hard-boiled egg	coating
	fat for frying

1 Heat margarine in a saucepan.
2 Stir in flour and cook for several minutes.
3 Take pan off the heat and add tomato juice.
4 Return to heat and bring slowly to the boil.
5 Continue boiling until thick.
6 Add chopped hard-boiled egg and breadcrumbs.
7 Let mixture cool, then taste and season well.
8 Form into cutlet shapes, brush with a little milk and toss in crisp breadcrumbs.
9 Fry until crisp and brown.
10 Drain well.

Variation

Meat cutlets – use exactly the same method as for the above recipe but substitute 2–3 oz. cooked minced meat or flaked corned beef for the hard-boiled eggs. You can use ¼ pint milk or stock instead of the tomato juice (2 servings).

Devilled eggs (1)

cooking time: 30 minutes

you will need:

6 hard-boiled eggs	2 oz. celery, finely
little milk	chopped (optional)
Worcestershire	1 oz. flour
sauce	1 teaspoon sugar
made mustard	pepper and salt
2 oz. butter	1 lb. tomatoes
1 small chopped	breadcrumbs
onion	

1 Cut eggs in halves lengthwise and remove yolks.
2 Press these through a sieve.
3 Moisten them with a little milk and flavour with Worcestershire sauce and mustard.
4 Refill whites with this mixture.
5 Melt butter over low heat.
6 Add onion and celery and cook until onion is transparent.
7 Blend in flour, sugar and seasonings.
8 Heat the skinned, roughly chopped tomatoes and gradually add these to the butter and flour mixture, stirring constantly.
9 Cook until thickened.
10 Pour mixture into a buttered shallow baking dish.
11 Arrange devilled eggs in the sauce and top with crumbs.
12 Place in a hot oven until sauce is bubbly round the edges for 10–15 minutes.
13 Serve with cooked rice, spaghetti, noodles or on toast.

Devilled eggs (2)

no cooking

you will need:

6 hard-boiled eggs	1 tablespoon
3 tablespoons cream	Worcestershire
½ tablespoon	sauce
softened butter	¼ teaspoon dry
½ teaspoon minced	mustard
parsley	little salt

1 Halve hard-boiled eggs lengthwise and remove yolks.
2 Mix yolks with other ingredients.
3 Fill egg-white shells with this mixture.
4 Serve on bed of lettuce and sprinkle the eggs with a little finely chopped spring onion or chives.

Devilled mushroom and egg

cooking time: 15 minutes

you will need:

2 oz. butter	ketchup
2 oz. mushrooms	1 teaspoon
good pinch curry	Worcestershire
powder	sauce
½ teaspoon made	3 hard-boiled eggs
mustard	4 rounds toast
1 teaspoon mustard	

1 Heat butter and fry chopped mushrooms in it, add flavourings.
2 When mushrooms are cooked, add quartered hard-boiled eggs.
3 Heat and serve at once on toast.

Eggs royale

cooking time: 15–20 minutes

you will need:

1 can condensed	1 onion
chicken or	2 oz. butter
celery soup	1 green pepper (or
little milk	cooked peas)
4 oz. grated cheese	5 hard-boiled eggs
1 small packet	olives
frozen beans	toast

1 Heat the soup with just a little milk, add the cheese and the beans, which should be lightly cooked so they still retain a slightly firm texture.
2 Slice and fry the onion in the butter, then add the chopped pepper.
3 When tender, stir into the soup mixture together with 4 of the chopped hard-boiled eggs.
4 Arrange in a casserole and garnish with the last egg and sliced stuffed olives, and border with triangles of crisp toast.

Fried devilled eggs

cooking time: 15 minutes

you will need:

6–8 hard-boiled	little milk or
eggs	mayonnaise for
2 teaspoons made	preference
mustard	pinch curry powder
salt	1 extra egg
pepper	breadcrumbs for
1 teaspoon	coating
Worcestershire	deep fat
sauce	

1 Cut hard-boiled eggs into halves lengthways.

2 Remove the yolks carefully, mash, adding the flavourings, and mayonnaise to make a soft consistency.

3 Press the filling back into the egg-white shells and 'join' the 2 halves together again.

4 Roll in the beaten egg, then in the crumbs.

5 Fry until crisp and golden brown.

Variation

Devilled eggs in duffle coats – follow above recipe to stage 3.

Wrap a slice of streaky bacon round each 'joined' egg, pressing overlapping bacon well together. Continue as above.

Monte Carlo eggs

cooking time: 30 minutes

you will need:

1 lb. spinach	½ oz. butter
(fresh or frozen)	4 eggs
seasoning	

for sauce:

½ oz. butter	seasoning
½ oz. flour	⅜ pint milk
1½ oz. cheese	

1 Prepare spinach and wash in several waters.

2 Cook until tender in a very little water. Add seasoning.

3 Drain and press well.

4 Reheat with a little butter and place on the bottom of a soufflé dish.

5 Press in the lightly boiled (5 minutes) shelled eggs.

6 Cover with the cheese sauce.

7 Sprinkle over a little more cheese and brown under the grill or heat through in the oven with water round.

Oeufs Mirabeau

cooking time: 3–4 minutes

you will need:

hard-boiled eggs	pepper
butter	parsley, finely chopped
salt	

1 Shell hard-boiled eggs.

2 Cut them in slices and fry lightly in butter (without letting the butter brown).

3 Serve the eggs sprinkled with salt, pepper and parsley.

Scotch eggs

cooking time: 40–45 minutes

you will need:

2 eggs	little beaten egg
8 oz. sausage meat	breadcrumbs to coat

1 Hard-boil the eggs.

2 Wrap them carefully in the sausage meat to make a neat shape.

3 Brush with a little egg or milk and roll in crisp breadcrumbs.

4 Bake on a greased tin in the centre of a moderate oven (375°F. – Gas Mark 4) for 30 minutes, or fry.

5 Serve hot or cold.

Cheddar Scotch eggs

cooking time: 15–25 minutes

you will need:

4 hard-boiled eggs	little chopped chives
3 oz. grated	or spring onions
Cheddar cheese	seasoning
tiny knob butter	12 oz. sausage meat

for coating:

little flour	breadcrumbs
1 egg	deep fat for frying

1 Cut hard-boiled eggs into halves very carefully and remove yolk.

2 Put yolk into basin, mash and add cheese, butter, chives, seasoning.

3 Mix well and press back into white cases. Press the two halves together.

4 Divide sausage meat into 4 portions. Flatten on lightly floured board.

5 Put egg on to this, then wrap egg round with sausage meat.

6 Seal 'joints' very firmly.

7 Coat with beaten egg – roll in crumbs.

8 Fry **steadily** in deep fat until golden brown or brush with little melted fat – put on to hot greased tin and bake in moderately hot oven (400°F. – Gas Mark 5) for 25 minutes.

9 Drain very well on absorbent paper.

10 Serve hot with vegetables.

11 Serve cold with salad for a picnic dish.

Creamy Scotch eggs

cooking time: 35 minutes

you will need:

4 eggs	little chopped chives
3 oz. cream cheese	or spring onions
tiny knob butter	seasoning
	1 lb. sausage meat

for coating:

little flour	breadcrumbs
1 egg	fat for frying

1 Hard-boil eggs and cut into halves very carefully.
2 Remove yolks, put into basin, mash and add cream cheese, butter, chives, seasoning.
3 Mix well and press back into white cases, press the two halves together.
4 Divide sausage meat into 4 portions.
5 Flatten on lightly floured board, put egg on to this then wrap round in sausage meat.
6 Seal 'joins' very firmly.
7 Coat with beaten egg – roll in crumbs.
8 Fry **steadily** in deep fat until golden brown **or** brush with little melted fat – put on to hot greased tin and bake in moderately hot oven (400°F. – Gas Mark 5) for 25 minutes.
9 Drain very well on absorbent paper.

Scrambled eggs

cooking time: 8 minutes

you will need for 1 good serving:

½ oz. margarine	2 tablespoons milk
or butter	seasoning
2 eggs	

1 Heat the margarine in a saucepan.
2 Beat the eggs and milk together and season well.
3 Pour this into the hot fat and cook as slowly as possible until the eggs are **just** set. Stir all the time with a wooden spoon.

Note

If scrambled eggs are cooked too quickly, they will curdle and appear 'watery' at the bottom of the pan.

Variations

A well cooked scrambled egg on toast is delicious – and there are many ways in which it can be varied:

Scrambled eggs with chicken – heat any tiny scraps of cooked chicken in the milk and butter, then add the beaten seasoned egg and cook until just set.

Scrambled eggs with ham – heat any tiny scraps of ham in the milk and butter, but as ham is slightly salty reduce quantity in seasoning. Then add the beaten seasoned egg and cook until just set.

Scrambled eggs with bacon and macaroni or spaghetti – fry the bacon in the pan until really crisp, then add a little cooked and well-drained macaroni or chopped spaghetti. Heat for a minute, add the eggs and cook until just set.

Scrambled eggs with prawns or shrimps – toss the prawns or shrimps in the hot butter or margarine, add the seasoned and well-beaten eggs with a little top of the milk or cream, and cook until just set. Do not be too generous with the salt.

Scrambled eggs with tomatoes – use recipe for scrambled eggs. Allow a good-sized tomato for each 2 eggs. Skin and slice thinly and heat in the butter. Beat eggs, add to tomato, season and cook until just set.

Scrambled egg with mushrooms – fry thinly sliced mushroom stalks until very soft in margarine, then add finely chopped mushroom heads. When quite tender, add to lightly scrambled eggs.

It is better to cook the eggs in a separate pan, otherwise you spoil the colour.

Scrambled eggs with fried bread and onions – use recipe for scrambled eggs. Chop an onion finely and cook in the hot butter until soft, then add a few cubes of bread and brown these. Add the beaten eggs and cook until just set.

Plain omelette

cooking time: 5–8 minutes

you will need per person:

1½–2 eggs	1 tablespoon water
good pinch salt	knob butter
and pepper	

1 Beat eggs in a basin.
2 Add salt and pepper and water to eggs and mix well.
3 Put a knob of butter into an omelette pan and when hot pour in eggs.

4 Leave for about 1 minute over high heat to allow bottom to set, then loosen egg mixture from sides of pan and cook rapidly, tipping pan from side to side so that the liquid egg flows underneath and cooks quickly.

5 When egg is set, slip palette knife under omelette and fold it away from handle of pan.

6 Grasp handle firmly and tip on to a hot plate.

Variations

Leek and bacon – mix diced cooked bacon and chopped cooked leek together and fill omelette just before serving.

Leek and tomato – skin and simmer chopped tomatoes in a little butter until a smooth purée, season well. Add chopped cooked leeks and heat in the tomato purée. Fill cooked omelette with this mixture just before serving.

Anchovy omelette – make a plain omelette (see above) and garnish with anchovy fillets.

Corned beef omelette – use recipe and method for plain omelette (see above) but use a little more butter in the pan. Flake the beef and blend with the beaten eggs before cooking.

Corn on the cob omelette – use recipe and method for plain omelette (see above). To each 2 eggs add 2 tablespoons cooked or canned corn. Add the corn to the beaten eggs before cooking.

Omelette Americaine

cooking time: 10–15 minutes

you will need per person:

little butter	1 teaspoon chives,
1 rasher bacon,	chopped
diced	seasoning
1 tomato	2 eggs

1 Heat the butter in a small pan, then add diced bacon and fry until crisp and golden brown.

2 Add skinned sliced tomato, chives and seasoning and cook until it forms a good purée.

3 Make the omelette in the usual way (see above) and fill with this mixture when nearly set.

Bacon and cheese omelette

you will need per person:

1 rasher bacon,	1 oz. grated cheese
diced	2 eggs

1 Fry the bacon until crisp.

2 Add cooked bacon and cheese to the beaten eggs and cook in the usual way.

Kidney omelette

cooking time: 10–15 minutes

you will need:

for filling:

2 kidneys	1 oz. butter
1 oz. flour	¼ pint stock
salt and pepper	

for plain omelette:

4 eggs	1 oz. butter
salt and pepper	

1 Prepare the kidneys by removing outer skin and washing them well. Slice and toss in the seasoned flour.

2 Melt butter in a saucepan, put in the kidneys and fry for a few minutes.

3 Add the rest of the flour and the stock. Cook until thickened.

4 Beat up the eggs.

5 Season, melt butter in an omelette pan or saucepan and pour in the egg mixture.

6 When it starts to set, tilt the pan so that the uncooked mixture runs to the sides.

7 When the omelette is set, fill with the kidney sauce, fold in half and turn out on a hot dish.

Macaroni omelette

cooking time: 10 minutes

you will need for 2–3 servings:

3 eggs	2 rashers bacon,
seasoning	diced
2 oz. cooked short	good knob butter
cut macaroni or	2 tomatoes
spaghetti	parsley
2 oz. grated cheese	

1 Beat the eggs, season well.

2 Beat in cooked macaroni or short cut spaghetti and cheese.

3 Fry the diced bacon gently in the omelette pan.

4 Add the butter and when hot pour in the well seasoned egg mixture.

5 Allow to set at the bottom.

6 Tilt the pan and move the egg backwards and forwards, so the omelette cooks as quickly as possible.

7 Fold and serve with the sliced tomatoes and chopped parsley to garnish.

Fish and potato omelette

cooking time: 10 minutes

you will need for 2 servings:

2 eggs
2 tablespoons milk
salt
pepper

8 oz. flaked cooked
fish
2 oz. cooked mashed
potato
1 oz. butter

1 Whisk eggs and milk together, season well.
2 Add fish and pour on to the potato.
3 Mix lightly together.
4 Melt butter in omelette pan and pour in the fish mixture.
5 Cook until set underneath and then set top under a hot grill.
6 Fold over and serve immediately.

Welsh omelette

cooking time: 20 minutes

you will need:

2 sliced leeks
6 rashers bacon,
chopped
2 large raw potatoes,
diced

butter for frying
salt and pepper
8 eggs
4 oz. grated cheese

1 Fry the leeks, bacon and potatoes in hot butter.
2 Divide this mixture into four. Season well.
3 Use two seasoned beaten eggs for each omelette, cooking them in the usual way (see page 40).
4 When cooked, sprinkle with a quarter of the mixture then cover with grated cheese.
5 Put the frying pan under a hot grill until the cheese is golden.
6 Serve each omelette without folding.

Chinese omelettes

These appear on Chinese menus and often are used to garnish another dish. The thin omelette is made by using a very small number of eggs so that a wafer-thin layer (like a pancake) is poured over the hot oil, then cooked until firm, removed from the pan, folded, then shredded evenly.

Even when Chinese omelettes are filled, they are thinner, firmer and less light than the French variety.

Leek omelette

you will need per person:

1 or 2 cooked
leeks
little butter

plain omelette (see
page 40)
1–2 oz. grated cheese

1 Heat the cooked leeks in the butter and keep hot while the omelette is cooked, adding grated cheese at the last minute.
2 Put the leek and cheese mixture into the omelette just before serving.

Omelette Indienne

cooking time: 5–8 minutes

you will need per person:

plain omelette (see
page 40)
½–1 teaspoon curry
powder

cooked rice
curry sauce (see
page 13)

1 Cook the omelette in the usual way.
2 Fill with a little curried cooked rice.
3 Serve with curry sauce (see page 13).

Omelette Italienne

cooking time: 5–8 minutes

you will need per person:

small rasher bacon
little butter
1 chicken's liver
1–2 mushrooms

seasoning
plain omelette (see
page 40)

1 Chop the bacon and fry until golden.
2 Add butter and toss the chopped liver and diced mushrooms in this for a few minutes.
3 Season well and use as filling for the cooked plain omelette.

Asparagus omelette

cooking time: 5 minutes

you will need per person:

asparagus – fresh
or canned
2 eggs
salt and pepper

1 level teaspoon
cornflour
2 teaspoons milk
¼ oz. butter

1 Have the asparagus ready and keep it hot whilst making the omelette.
2 Beat the eggs lightly with the salt and pepper.
3 Mix the cornflour smoothly with the milk and add to the eggs.
4 Heat the butter in a thick frying pan.
5 Pour in the egg mixture and work omelette in the usual way.

6 When cooked put in a few spears of asparagus in the middle and fold forming a cushion shape.

7 Turn on to a hot dish and serve at once with the remaining asparagus.

Pancakes

Basic batter for pancakes

cooking time: 3–5 minutes

you will need:

4 oz. flour	½ pint milk or milk
pinch salt	and water
1 egg	

1 Sieve flour and salt. Make a well in the centre.
2 Add the egg and mix in enough milk to give a sticky consistency. Beat until smooth.
3 Gradually add rest of liquid.

Rich pancake batter

cooking time: 3–5 minutes

you will need:

4 oz. flour	2 eggs
pinch salt	just under ½ pint
1 tablespoon olive oil	milk or milk and
	water

Use method as above, adding the oil last of all.

Pancakes with shrimp sauce

cooking time: 12–15 minutes

you will need:

pancake batter
   (see above)

for sauce:

¾ oz. butter	squeeze lemon juice
¾ oz. cornflour	anchovy essence
½ pint milk	seasoning
1 dessertspoon	4 oz. fresh or frozen
tomato purée	shrimps

1 Make pancakes and fill with sauce made as follows.
2 Melt the butter in a pan.
3 Add the cornflour and mix well and cook for 1 minute, stirring, then gradually add milk and boil until thickened.
4 Add tomato purée, lemon juice, anchovy essence and seasoning to taste. Do **not** allow to boil.

5 Finally add the drained shrimps and keep hot till required.

Savoury pancakes

cooking time: 8–10 minutes

you will need:

for filling:

1 tablespoon corn oil	1 hard-boiled egg
½ oz. cornflour	4 oz. cooked ham
½ pint milk	1 teaspoon chopped
1 stick celery	parsley

for pancakes:

3 oz. plain flour	1 egg
1 oz. cornflour	½ pint milk
pinch salt	corn oil for frying

to make the filling:

1 Heat the corn oil.
2 Add the cornflour and cook for 1 minute.
3 Stir in the milk, bring to the boil and boil for 3 minutes, stirring all the time.
4 Add all the other chopped ingredients and cook for a further 1 minute to heat through.

to make pancakes:

1 Sieve the flour, cornflour and salt into a basin.
2 Make a well in the centre and add the egg and some of the milk.
3 Beat until a smooth batter is formed.
4 Stir in the remainder of the milk and leave to stand for as long as possible.
5 Heat the corn oil in a small frying pan and cook the pancakes in the usual way.
6 Place spoonfuls of the filling into each pancake and fold up.
7 Garnish with parsley.

More fillings for savoury pancakes

With chicken – finely diced chicken in a creamy sauce – coated with more cream or cheese sauce.

With minced beef – chopped minced beef, mixed with fried onions and tomatoes.

With liver – finely diced liver, fried with chopped mushrooms.

With fish – flaked cooked white or shellfish in a creamy white sauce – garnished with shellfish and served with extra sauce.

Pancake rolls

cooking time: 20 minutes

you will need:

2 onions, chopped
1 oz. dripping
1 oz. plain flour
½ pint stock or
  hot water
2 beef extract
  cubes
1 tablespoon tomato
  purée or ketchup

8 oz. cooked minced
  beef
salt and pepper
pancake batter (see
  page 43)
parsley

1 Lightly fry the onions in hot dripping and add the flour.
2 Cook for 1 minute.
3 Add the stock slowly, stirring continuously. Add the beef cubes and stir until dissolved.
4 Stir in the tomato purée, salt and pepper and continue to cook for a further few minutes.
5 Add meat to this sauce and keep hot for filling each pancake as it is cooked.
6 Cook pancakes in the usual way (see page 43), fill and serve hot with chopped parsley.

Ham pancakes

cooking time: 2–3 minutes for each pancake

you will need:

basic pancake batter
  (see page 43)
8 thin slices ham
  (about size of your
  pancake pan)

sliced tomatoes
1–2 mushrooms
parsley

1 Make the pancake batter and fry on one side.
2 Turn and arrange the slice of ham on this cooked side on the pan while the other side cooks.
3 Roll firmly and serve with sliced cooked tomatoes, mushrooms and parsley to garnish.

Cheese Dishes

With the great variety of cheeses available today, your cheese savouries should never be monotonous. Cheese is a food that is not only spoilt in flavour if over-cooked, but is made very difficult to digest by prolonged cooking. It is better to prepare your supper snacks which use cheese and then do the final cooking just before serving.

Spinach and cheese mould

cooking time: 2–3 minutes for each pancake plus 8 minutes

you will need:

about 12 oz. cooked
  spinach purée
½ pint cheese sauce
  (see page 83)

basic pancake mixture
  (see page 43)
2 oz. cheese, grated

1 Heat and season the spinach purée well.
2 Make cheese sauce.
3 Cook pancakes, put on to a hot dish.
4 Sandwich each pancake with a layer of spinach purée and sprinkling of cheese.
5 When all the pancakes have been cooked, coat with the cheese sauce, sprinkling any remaining cheese on top.
6 Put for about 8 minutes into a hot oven (450°F. – Gas Mark 7).
7 Cut into slices to serve.

Cheese aigrettes

cooking time: 10–15 minutes

you will need:

1 oz. butter or
  margarine
¼ pint water
2 oz. flour
1½ oz. cheese,
  finely grated

good pinch salt
cayenne pepper
2 egg yolks
deep fat for frying
cheese to garnish

1 Put the butter and water into a saucepan and bring to the boil.
2 Heat until butter has melted.
3 Stir in the flour and continue heating, stirring all the time, until the mixture leaves the sides of the pan.
4 Take off the heat and add the grated cheese, seasoning and the well-beaten egg yolks.
5 Let the mixture become quite cold.
6 Drop small spoonfuls of the mixture into very hot fat, immediately turning the heat as low as possible to prevent aigrettes becoming too brown on the outside before cooking through to the middle.
7 When crisp and brown, drain carefully on absorbent paper and pile on to hot dish.
8 Sprinkle with seasoning and a little more grated cheese.

Ham and cheese cream flan

cooking time: 30–35 minutes

you will need:

4 oz. short crust or flaky pastry (see page 70)	2 teaspoons chopped chives **or** spring onion tops, chopped finely
2 eggs	little chopped parsley
4 oz. cottage or cream cheese	little cream or milk
6 oz. ham*	seasoning
	little chopped gherkin

*3 oz. must be in nice slices

1 Line a rather shallow 6½ or 7-inch flan ring or tin with the pastry and bake 'blind' for approximately 15 minutes in a hot oven (450°F. – Gas Mark 7) – even a little hotter for flaky pastry. By this time the pastry should be set, but not brown.
2 Beat the eggs into 3 oz. of the cheese.
3 Add 3 oz. chopped ham, the chives, little parsley and enough cream or milk to give a soft mixture.
4 Season well and put into the flan case.
5 Bake for a further 15 minutes in a moderately hot oven (400°F. – Gas Mark 5) until the pastry is brown and the filling is firm.
6 Allow to cool then garnish with tiny ham rolls made by cutting into neat pieces, spreading with the rest of the cream cheese, mixed with a few drops milk, chopped parsley and gherkin.
7 Serve with salad.

Variation

Celery and cheese cream flan – use the above recipe but substitute 4 sticks of celery for the ham. Finely chop 3 of the sticks of celery, and mix into 3 oz. of the cheese and the eggs instead of ham. To garnish cut remaining stick of celery into 1½ inch pieces and fill with the cream cheese mixed with milk and flavouring.

Savoury soufflés

cooking time: 35–40 minutes

you will need:

for sauce:

1 oz. butter	4 eggs or 3 yolks and 5 whites
1 oz. flour	flavouring
¼–⅓ pint milk	seasoning

1 Make a white sauce with the butter, flour and milk.

2 Beat in the egg yolks.
3 Add flavouring and seasoning.
4 Fold in stiffly beaten egg whites.
5 Put into a 6-inch buttered soufflé dish and bake in the centre of a moderate oven (375°F. – Gas Mark 4) until golden brown and well risen.

Flavourings

Cheese – use 4 oz. grated cheese and sprinkle some on top before baking.
Cheese and ham – use half grated cheese and half chopped ham.
Purée – use spinach or tomato purée instead of milk for the sauce.
Fish – use 5 oz. flaked white or canned fish.
Chicken – use 5 oz. finely chopped, cold shredded chicken, duck, etc.

Cheese and vegetable soufflé

cooking time: 25–30 minutes

you will need:

8 oz. cooked mixed vegetables	pepper
½ pint milk or vegetable stock	1 teaspoon already mixed mustard
1 oz. semolina	1 oz. grated cheese
1 egg	1 level teaspoon baking powder
salt	

1 Butter a casserole dish.
2 Put vegetables in the bottom of casserole dish.
3 Boil the milk, sprinkle in semolina, stirring all the time.
4 Boil for 7 minutes to make sure the semolina is cooked.
5 Cool slightly and add egg, seasoning and mustard.
6 Lastly, add cheese with baking powder, mix thoroughly.
7 Place the mixture on top of the vegetables in the casserole and sprinkle with a little grated cheese.
8 Cook in hot oven (425–450°F. – Gas Mark 6–7).

Golden cheese tart

cooking time: 40 minutes

you will need:

6 oz. short crust pastry (see page 70)	2 oz. finely grated Parmesan cheese or rather strong Cheddar cheese
1 oz. butter or margarine	1 can sweet corn
8 oz. soft cream cheese or cottage cheese	2 grated raw carrots
	2 or 3 tablespoons milk

to garnish:

tomato	cucumber

1 Bake pastry 'blind' in flan tin until golden in colour.
2 Cream the fat with the cream cheese.
3 Add all the other ingredients.
4 Put into the flan case and serve topped with slices of cucumber and tomato.
5 If you would like this as a hot dish, garnish with tomato slices round the edge of the flan and put into moderate oven (375°F. – Gas Mark 4) for 15 minutes.

Spinach soufflé

cooking time: 35–40 minutes

you will need:

12 oz.–1 lb. cooked spinach	seasoning
1 oz. butter	3–4 eggs
1 oz. flour	2 oz. grated Parmesan cheese (optional)
$\frac{1}{8}$ pint milk	

1 Chop the spinach finely or put it through a sieve.
2 Heat butter, stir in flour, cook for several minutes, then add milk, spinach purée and seasoning.
3 Beat in egg yolks and cheese and stiffly beaten egg whites.
4 Pour into 6-inch soufflé dish and bake in centre of moderate oven (375°F. – Gas Mark 4).

Variation

Carrot soufflé – use recipe for spinach soufflé above but use 8 oz. carrots which can be cooked and sieved, but which are delicious if used raw and grated. Add pinch of nutmeg to ingredients if liked.

Cheese, onion and potato pie

cooking time: 45 minutes

you will need:

4 medium sized potatoes	2 medium sized onions

for sauce:

$\frac{1}{2}$ oz. butter	4 oz. Cheddar cheese, grated
$\frac{1}{2}$ oz. flour	salt
$\frac{1}{4}$ pint milk	pepper

1 Peel potatoes and slice thinly.
2 Skin onions and slice thinly. Separate into rings.
3 Grease small heatproof casserole and build up alternate layers of sliced potato and onion.
4 Make sauce by melting butter, stir in flour and cook for 1 minute.
5 Remove from heat and gradually add milk, stirring all the time.
6 Return to heat, bring to boil stirring until sauce thickens.
7 Add 3 oz. cheese and seasoning, stir until cheese melts and pour over potatoes and onions.
8 Top with remaining grated cheese.
9 Bake in a moderately hot oven (400°F. – Gas Mark 5) until potatoes are cooked.

Cheese potatoes

no cooking

you will need:

6 new potatoes, cooked	seasoning
2 oz. cream cheese	few cornflakes

1 Cut the potatoes into halves.
2 Pipe or spread cheese over the top. Season well.
3 Decorate with crushed cornflakes.

Cheese and potato balls

cooking time: 1 or 2 minutes for each batch of balls

you will need:

4 oz. mashed potato (kept fairly dry)	good pinch salt, pepper and mustard
4 oz. finely grated cheese	1 teaspoon finely chopped parsley
	little flour
	oil for frying

1 Mix all the ingredients together, making the mixture into small balls.
2 Roll balls in flour.

3 Heat the oil and fry the balls until crisp and brown. If using deep fat, it is advisable to dip the balls into the boiling fat for ½ minute only, remove them for ½ minute and bring the fat to boiling point again, then continue cooking.
4 Serve with a green vegetable and cheese or tomato sauce (see pages 83, 84).

Variation

Cheese, bacon and potato balls – make recipe as above but instead of 4 oz. finely grated cheese, only use 2 oz. plus 2 oz. finely chopped cooked bacon.

Cheese pudding

cooking time: 30–35 minutes

you will need:

½ pint milk	4 oz. grated cheese
1 oz. butter or margarine	seasoning
4 oz. breadcrumbs	1 or 2 eggs

1 Bring the milk to the boil.
2 Add the butter or margarine, and breadcrumbs and stand on one side for 5 minutes.
3 Add the cheese and season well.
4 Stir in the eggs.
5 Pour into a well-greased dish and bake in the centre of a hot oven (450°F. – Gas Mark 7) until brown on top.
6 Serve at once with baked tomatoes.

Variations

Cream cheese pudding – use recipe for cheese pudding (see above) but use 6 oz. cream cheese instead of grated cheese. Put the cream cheese in a basin and gradually add the boiling milk, stirring until smoothly blended. Finish as above.

Cheese and bacon pudding – use recipe for cheese pudding, but fry 2 or 3 finely chopped rashers of bacon and add to the mixture. Use 2 eggs to make this pudding really light.

Cheese and haddock pudding – use recipe for cheese pudding but use 4 oz. flaked cooked smoked haddock and 1½ oz. grated Parmesan cheese.

Cheese rolls

cooking time: 12 minutes

you will need:

8 oz. self-raising flour	1 oz. margarine
salt, pepper, mustard	3 oz. cheese, finely grated
	milk

1 Sieve flour with good pinch of salt, pepper and mustard.
2 Rub in margarine.
3 Add cheese and enough milk to bind.
4 Make into finger shapes and brush top with milk.
5 Bake for approximately 12 minutes towards top of hot oven.
6 Halve and fill with salad, with ham or other cold meat.

Cheese and walnut loaf

cooking time: 45 minutes–1 hour

you will need:

8 oz. plain flour	4 oz. margarine
2 level teaspoons baking powder	4 oz. Cheddar cheese, grated
1 level teaspoon dry mustard	1 oz. walnuts, chopped
1 level teaspoon salt	2 eggs, beaten
good pinch pepper	¼ pint milk

1 Well grease a 2-lb. loaf tin.
2 Sieve together the plain flour, baking powder, mustard, salt and pepper.
3 Rub in the margarine lightly until the mixture resembles fine crumbs.
4 Add the cheese and walnuts.
5 Mix to a soft dropping consistency with the beaten eggs and milk.
6 Turn into the prepared tin and bake in the centre of moderately hot oven (400°F. – Gas Mark 5).
7 Turn on to a cake wire to cool. When cold, cut into slices and spread with butter.

Note

This loaf is wonderful with cheese and salad.

Variations

Cheese and tomato loaf – use recipe for cheese and walnut loaf, but omit the walnuts and bind with tomato juice instead of milk.

Cheese seed loaf – use recipe for cheese and walnut loaf but use a dessertspoon of carraway seeds instead of walnuts.

Cheese and rice croquettes

cooking time: 25–30 minutes

you will need:

4 oz. rice	seasoning
6 oz. cheese, finely grated	1 egg white
little parsley, chopped	fine breadcrumbs
1 egg yolk	fat for frying

1 Cook rice in slightly salted water and drain very well.
2 Mix with the cheese, chopped parsley and egg yolk. Season.
3 Form into finger shapes and use the egg white for coating them.
4 Roll in fine crumbs and deep fry or bake in the oven until golden.

Variation

Cheese and potato croquettes – use recipe above, but use 8 oz. mashed potatoes instead of the rice.

Savoury fruit batter

cooking time: 25–30 minutes

you will need:

2 oz. plain flour	¼ pint milk
¼ level teaspoon nutmeg	½ oz. butter
pinch salt	3 oz. Cheddar cheese, grated
1 egg	2 oz. sultanas

1 Sieve together flour, nutmeg and salt, make a well in centre.
2 Add egg and gradually add milk, stirring well until batter is smooth.
3 Beat well, cover and leave to stand for at least ½ hour.
4 Place butter in 1-pint pie dish and heat in oven until hot.
5 Sprinkle cheese and sultanas in bottom of pie dish, pour in batter.
6 Bake in a hot oven (425–450°F. – Gas Mark 6–7). Serve at once.

Variation

Surprise fruit batter – make recipe as above but instead of cheese and sultanas substitute 4 rings of apple. Before serving, sprinkle pudding with sugar.

Pizzas

cooking time: 20 minutes

you will need:

for yeast dough:

1 lb. plain flour	1 teaspoon sugar
2 level teaspoons salt	approximately ½ pint water
½ oz. yeast	1 tablespoon oil

for filling:

2 tablespoons olive oil	½ teaspoon oregano (dried herb) for an extra Italian flavour
1 medium onion	
1 clove garlic	6 oz. finely grated Cheddar, Cheshire, Gruyère or Mozzarella cheese
1 lb. peeled tomatoes or drained canned tomatoes	
salt and pepper to taste	

for topping:

slices salami	black olives
hard-boiled eggs	

1 Sieve flour and salt into large bowl.
2 Cream yeast and sugar, add ¼ pint tepid water, put into warm place for 10 minutes.
3 Add the yeast liquid to the flour with oil and sufficient water to make a soft dough.
4 Knead the dough by pulling it up and pressing it down on a lightly floured board until it feels smooth, firm and elastic – about 5 minutes.
5 Prepare filling by frying finely chopped onion and garlic in hot oil and then adding sliced tomatoes and seasoning.
6 Shape the dough into a ball.
7 Place in a greased polythene bag, lightly tied, or a large greased pan and cover.
8 Put to rise in a warm place until double in size.
9 Then knead the dough lightly and flatten, with the knuckles or a rolling pin, to a long strip.
10 Brush with oil and roll up like a Swiss roll.
11 Repeat this three times in all.
12 Divide the dough into 6 pieces and roll each piece to a flat circle to fit greased sponge tins (this quantity makes six 6-inch pizzas).
13 Brush the dough with oil and cover with filling.
14 Top with grated cheese, then with slices of salami, sliced hard-boiled eggs and black olives.
15 Bake for 15 to 20 minutes towards top of a hot oven (450°F. – Gas Mark 7).

Cheese batter

cooking time: 20–35 minutes

you will need:

for batter:

4 oz. flour	½ pint milk
pinch salt	little fat
1 egg	2 oz. cheese, grated

for filling:

½ pint thick cheese sauce (see page 83)	8 oz. cooked diced vegetables
	seasoning
	parsley

1 Sieve the flour with a pinch of salt into a basin.
2 Add the egg and gradually beat in the milk.
3 Heat the fat in a Yorkshire pudding tin, or use 4 individual dishes, and pour in the batter. The cheese should be stirred into this **just before** it goes into the cooking dish.
4 Cooking for 20 minutes for individual dishes and about 35 minutes for a large one, in a hot oven (450°F. – Gas Mark 7).
5 Meanwhile make the sauce.
6 Add the vegetables and seasoning.
7 Serve the batter and fill with the cheese and vegetable mixture.
8 Garnish with chopped parsley.

Pineapple and cream cheese pancakes

cooking time: 2–3 minutes for each pancake

you will need:

pancake batter (see page 43)	pineapple rings
butter	cream cheese
	cherries

1 Spread hot pancakes with butter, rings of pineapple and cream cheese.
2 Decorate with cherries.

Vegetable Dishes

There is a wonderful selection of vegetables available throughout the year which can be used as the basis for light savoury dishes of all kinds. In order to retain the maximum flavour and goodness of vegetables do not over-cook them.

Cauliflower and mushroom au gratin

cooking time: 30 minutes

you will need:

1 good sized cauliflower	seasoning
6–8 mushrooms	2–3 oz. cheese, grated
½ pint milk	2–3 tablespoons crumbs
1 oz. flour	melted butter
1 oz. butter	

1 Divide cauliflower into flowerets and cook in boiling salted water until just soft.
2 Meanwhile, simmer chopped mushrooms in milk until tender.
3 Blend flour and butter together into a paste with a knife.
4 Drop small pieces of this paste into the simmering mushroom mixture and whisk well. Season.
5 Continue stirring until smooth and thickened.
6 Pour into a shallow buttered dish.
7 Arrange cauliflower on top.
8 Sprinkle cheese and crumbs on top with melted butter and brown under grill.

Variations

Cauliflower and leeks au gratin – use cooked leeks instead of mushrooms.

Cauliflower and peppers au gratin – fry 2 or 3 chopped sweet red peppers in butter and use in place of mushrooms. Make the cheese sauce from 1 oz. butter, 1 oz. flour, ½ pint milk and 2 oz. of the cheese.

Corn fritters

cooking time: 5 minutes

you will need:

for batter:

2 oz. self-raising flour	5 tablespoons milk or milk and water
seasoning	4 oz. cooked sweet corn
½ egg, beaten (optional)	fat for frying

1 Make a batter with the flour, seasoning, egg (if used) and liquid (see page 43).
2 Beat well.
3 Stir in the corn and fry tablespoons of the mixture in a little hot fat until golden brown on both sides.

Cauliflower and tomato fritters

cooking time: 25 minutes

you will need:

1 small cauliflower	¼ pint tomato purée
4 oz. flour	or canned tomato
good pinch salt	juice
1 egg	fat or oil for frying
	cayenne pepper

1 Divide the cauliflower into neat sprigs – try to keep them as near the same size as possible.
2 Cook in boiling salted water until just soft, but unbroken.
3 Drain well.
4 Sieve the flour and salt together.
5 Add the well-beaten egg and gradually beat in the tomato purée or tomato juice.
6 Put the pieces of cauliflower into this batter and when well coated drop in boiling fat and cook until crisp and brown.
7 Dust with cayenne pepper and serve at once.

Variations

Cauliflower cheese fritters – use milk instead of tomato juice and add 2 oz. grated cheese to the batter.

Curried cauliflower fritters – add 2 teaspoons curry powder to the batter, sieving with the flour.

Mushroom fingers

cooking time: 10–15 minutes

you will need:

8 oz. mushrooms	dash Worcestershire
⅛ pint milk	sauce
1 oz. flour	little parsley, chopped
1 oz. butter	4 slices buttered
seasoning	toast

1 Wash and chop mushroom caps and stalks coarsely.
2 Simmer in the milk until tender.
3 Blend flour and butter together and work into mushroom mixture gradually.
4 Cook gently for some little time until smooth.
5 Season well, add sauce and parsley.
6 Spread on toast and divide into fingers.

Variation

Mushroom cheese fingers – use previous recipe, but add 4 oz. grated cheese. Proceed to step 4, add the cheese and cook until melted. Continue as before.

Stuffed mushrooms (1)

cooking time: 20–25 minutes

you will need:

8 really big	1 tiny onion
mushrooms, or 12	little parsley
smaller ones	seasoning
4 rashers bacon	little butter

1 Wash mushrooms and remove stalks.
2 Chop stalks and mix with the chopped bacon, onion and parsley.
3 Season well.
4 Press this mixture into the centre of each mushroom, cover with a little butter and greased paper.
5 Bake in the centre of a moderately hot oven (400°F. – Gas Mark 5).

Variation

Stuffed mushrooms (2) – use the chopped mushroom stalks, onion, 4 oz. breadcrumbs, pinch mixed herbs, 2 beaten eggs, and omit bacon.

Stuffed peppers

cooking time: 30 minutes

you will need:

4 green peppers

for stuffing:

2 onions	3 oz. cooked rice
3 tomatoes	seasoning
2 oz. margarine	little parsley, chopped

1 Halve the peppers lengthwise and remove seeds and hard centre.
2 Put into boiling salted water and cook for about 5 minutes only.
3 Take out and drain.
4 Meanwhile fry the chopped onions and tomatoes in the margarine, add to the rice, season well and put into the centre of the peppers.
5 Cover with greased paper, put into a well-greased dish and bake in the centre of a moderate oven (375°F. – Gas Mark 4). Sprinkle with parsley.

Variations

With cheese – add plenty of grated cheese to the above ingredients.

With minced meat – use minced meat as well as the onions and tomatoes, and only 1 or 2 oz. rice.

Stuffed celery

no cooking

you will need:

1 head celery	cooked meat or fish
2 oz. cream cheese	seasoning
1 tablespoon tomato	1 hard-boiled egg
sauce	yolk

1 Trim celery and separate the stalks.
2 Beat the cheese until soft and creamy.
3 Add tomato sauce, finely chopped meat and seasoning.
4 Stuff grooves of celery with this mixture and sprinkle the tops with egg yolk.

Curried new potatoes

cooking time: 20–25 minutes

you will need:

1 oz. margarine	2 tablespoons water
1 tablespoon	1 dessertspoon
onion, grated or	Worcestershire
finely chopped	sauce
½ teaspoon curry	12 small new potatoes,
powder	cooked

1 Heat the margarine in a saucepan and fry the onion and curry powder in this until cooked.
2 Stir in the water and sauce and bring to the boil.
3 Add the potatoes and toss over a low heat until covered with the curry mixture.
4 Serve hot or cold.

Jacket potatoes

cooking time: 1 hour

you will need:

even-sized old	filling (see below)
potatoes	

1 Scrub potatoes scrupulously, and dry. Prick with a fork.
2 Rub well with oiled tissue paper.
3 Bake in a moderately hot oven (375°F. – Gas Mark 4).
4 When cooked, knead potatoes slightly to let out steam and make them floury.
5 Cut tops off the potatoes, scoop out the centre pulp, put into a basin with grated cheese, chopped ham **or** fried bacon.
6 Season well and add a little butter.
7 Blend well, return to potato cases and reheat in the oven for a short time.

Ham and parsley jacket potatoes

cooking time: 1¼ hours

you will need:

4 large potatoes	4 oz. cooked ham,
¼ pint thick parsley	chopped
sauce* (see page 83)	bacon rolls and
4 oz. cheese, grated	parsley to garnish

*or use parsley sauce mix

1 Scrub the potatoes very well and prick with a fork.
2 Bake for 1 hour in a moderately hot oven (400°F. – Gas Mark 5).
3 When cooked, cut the potatoes in half and carefully scoop out the centre.
4 Make the parsley sauce.
5 Add the potato pulp and 3½ oz. cheese. Mix well.
6 Place the ham in the bottom of the potato cases and pile the potato mixture on top.
7 Sprinkle with the remaining cheese and bake for 10–15 minutes in a moderately hot oven.
8 Finally put under the grill to brown the top.
9 Garnish with bacon rolls and parsley.

Potato and prawn mornay

cooking time: 25 minutes

you will need:

1–1½ lb. creamed	3 oz. cheese, grated
potatoes	2 hard-boiled eggs
margarine, melted	½ pint prawns, shelled
½ pint white	1 oz. breadcrumbs
sauce* (see page 83)	

*or white sauce mix

1 Line the casserole at the bottom and sides with the creamed potatoes.
2 Brush with a little melted margarine and put into a hot oven for about 10 minutes to crisp.
3 Meanwhile, make the sauce, add most of the cheese, the chopped eggs and prawns.
4 Pour into the potato case and top with the crumbs, cheese and a little melted margarine.
5 Return to the oven for about 10–15 minutes to crisp the top.

Note

Do not overcook, otherwise the prawns will toughen.

Variations

Cauliflower and egg mornay – use recipe for

potato and prawn mornay (see page 51) but cook a large cauliflower lightly, then divide into flowerets. Add 1 or 2 finely chopped gherkins and 2 or 3 chopped hard-boiled eggs. Pile into the potato case and top with the cheese, crumbs and melted margarine. Cook as before. Cooking time: 35–45 minutes.

Macedoine of vegetables mornay – use recipe for potato and prawn mornay (see page 51) but instead of the prawns and eggs use about 1 lb. diced cooked vegetables. Add extra cheese, if possible, and cook as before. Cooking time: 35–40 minutes.

Spinach mornay – use recipe for potato and prawn mornay (see page 51) but instead of prawns use about 1 lb. spinach. This should be cooked, chopped and drained **very well.** Put into the potato case, cover with sliced hard-boiled eggs and the sauce, etc. and cook as before. Cooking time: 35–40 minutes.

Tomato cups

cooking time: 10–15 minutes

you will need:

4 large tomatoes	2 oz. cheese, grated
2 egg yolks	2 tablespoons
2 egg whites	breadcrumbs
	seasoning

1 Cut a slice from the top of each tomato and scoop out the centre pulp.
2 Cut this finely.
3 Whisk the egg yolks.
4 Add the tomato pulp, cheese and breadcrumbs and season well.
5 Pile this filling into the tomato cases.
6 Whip the egg whites until very stiff, adding a pinch of salt and pepper.
7 Pile on top of the tomato cases.
8 Put into the centre of a moderate oven (375°F. – Gas Mark 4) for a good 10 minutes.
9 Serve with hot buttered toast.

Variation

Tomato corn cups – make recipe as above but substitute 2 oz. sweet corn kernels for the 2 tablespoons breadcrumbs.

Tomato and spinach cups

cooking time: 10–15 minutes

you will need:

4 large tomatoes	1 tablespoon cream
1 oz. butter or	from top of milk
margarine	seasoning
1 teaspoon onion,	4 slices cheese, cut
finely chopped	just about the size
2 heaped tablespoons	of each tomato
cooked spinach (or	
frozen spinach)	

1 Cut a slice from the top of each tomato and scoop out the centre pulp.
2 Chop this finely.
3 Heat the margarine in a saucepan and fry the onion until soft.
4 Mix with the spinach, cream, seasoning and the tomato pulp.
5 Put this into the tomato cases.
6 Lay the slices of cheese on top and replace the 'lids'.
7 Put into the centre of a moderate oven (375°F. – Gas Mark 4).

Spinach ring

cooking time: 1 hour

you will need:

1 onion	2 eggs
1 oz. butter	2 oz. soft
about 1 pint	breadcrumbs
cooked spinach	seasoning
purée	

1 Chop onion very finely and fry in hot butter.
2 Add to the other ingredients, mixing well.
3 Put into well-greased ring mould.
4 Put a piece of foil or greased paper over it and stand in a pan of water.
5 Bake for approximately 1 hour in a very moderate oven (350°F. – Gas Mark 3) until quite firm.
6 Turn out carefully.
7 The centre of the ring can be filled with hard-boiled eggs, ham, mushrooms or mixed vegetables, in a creamy white or cheese sauce (see page 83).

Supper snacks using baked beans

Baked beans are an excellent source of vegetable protein and are easy to prepare. Most people like them and they are particularly popular with children and teenagers.

If you team them with protein foods, such as bacon, cheese or eggs, you then have a very substantial dish.

The recipes on the following pages show how baked beans can provide an endless variety of quick supper dishes.

Carnival gammon

cooking time: 15–20 minutes

you will need:

4 slices unsmoked gammon	salt, pepper sugar
1 oz. butter	4 large tomatoes
little made mustard	1 8-oz. can curried beans with sultanas

1 Rind and snip the edge of the gammon at ½-inch intervals.
2 Work together butter, mustard and seasoning.
3 Spread thickly on the slices of gammon.
4 Bake for 5 minutes in a moderately hot oven (400°F. – Gas Mark 5).
5 Skin tomatoes, cut top off each and scoop out centre.
6 Season cases with salt, pepper and sugar and fill with curried beans with sultanas.
7 Place a stuffed tomato on each slice of gammon and return to the oven for 10–15 minutes.

Kidney kebabs

cooking time: 20–25 minutes

you will need:

1 onion	1 slice bread
1 oz. lard	4 oz. button mushrooms
1 16-oz. can baked beans in tomato sauce	4 sheep's kidneys chopped parsley

1 Fry the finely chopped onion lightly in a little hot fat.
2 Empty the baked beans into a saucepan and add the drained onion and heat.
3 Meanwhile, fry the bread until golden brown in the same pan used for the onion, slice into four pieces and keep warm.
4 Thread the mushrooms and kidneys, halved and skinned, alternately on to small skewers.
5 Brush with melted fat and grill for approximately 10–15 minutes, turning frequently.
6 Place baked beans in a heated serving dish and sprinkle with chopped parsley.
7 Lay the skewers on top of the beans and place the croûtes around the edge.

Mixed kebabs

cooking time: 10–15 minutes

you will need:

8 oz. rump or fillet steak	a few tiny mushrooms melted butter
8 oz. lean lamb **or** 8 oz. veal	barbecue sauce

1 Cut meat into small cubes. Thread with the mushrooms on to four or more metal skewers.
2 Brush with melted butter and cook under a hot grill. Keep turning kebabs until meat is brown and tender.
3 Make barbecue sauce (see page 27) to which add a small can baked beans. Serve with jacket potatoes topped with butter.

Sweet and sour casserole

cooking time: 30 minutes

you will need:

2 oz. lard	salt and pepper
4 teaspoons sugar	1 cooking apple
4 lean pork chops	1 16-oz. can baked beans in tomato sauce
8 tablespoons sweet cider	

1 Heat the lard and sugar in a casserole until they begin to caramelise.
2 Fry chops for 3 minutes on each side until nicely browned, in the caramelled fat.
3 Drain off all fat that may be left in the pan.
4 Add cider and seasoning.
5 Cover and simmer for 10–15 minutes.
6 Core the apple and slice into 4 rings.
7 Lift the chops on to a plate.
8 Turn the baked beans into the pan and replace the chops with a ring of apple on each.
9 Cover and cook for a further 5 minutes, or until apple is tender.

Baked bean rarebit

1 Make Welsh rarebit (see page 83).
2 Cover with baked beans and tomato sauce.
3 Serve with grilled bacon and a green salad.

Baked bean loaf

cooking time: 20–25 minutes

you will need:

1 large white loaf	2 or 3 tomatoes
butter	8 oz. sausages or
1 16-oz. can baked	chipolatas
beans in tomato	parsley
sauce	

1 Cut the top off the loaf lengthwise.
2 Scoop out the inside.
3 Spread inside and outside of crust with butter.
4 Bake until crisp in a hot oven – about 7–10 minutes.
5 Heat the baked beans.
6 Peel and slice the tomatoes.
7 Fry sausages.
8 Fill the loaf in layers with the beans and tomatoes.
9 Slice the sausages diagonally, or if chipolatas are used slice in half.
10 Arrange these on top of the last layer of beans.
11 Garnish with chopped parsley.

Bean and beef pie

cooking time: approximately 30 minutes

you will need:

1 oz. dripping	seasoning
1 large sliced onion	5 oz. can baked beans
2 skinned tomatoes	1–1½ lb. mashed
12 oz. cooked minced	potatoes
meat	1 oz. margarine
¼ pint gravy	

1 Fry onion and tomato in hot dripping until tender but not brown.
2 Add meat, gravy and seasoning.
3 Pour into a pie dish.
4 Add a layer of baked beans.
5 Cover with mashed potatoes. Rough up with a fork.
6 Dot with margarine and bake until golden brown (400°F. – Gas Mark 5).

Salads and Salad Dressings

A salad can make a quick savoury dish into a satisfying and appetising-looking meal, but it can also provide a sustaining meal in itself. Use some of the less 'every day' ingredients in your salads from time to time – chicory, red and green peppers, etc.

Add a salad dressing, which gives extra flavour and interest.

Bacon salad

no cooking

you will need:

8 oz. cooked bacon*	few capers
celery	mayonnaise (see page 57)
2 apples	
raw carrot	lettuce
cucumber	2 hard-boiled eggs
beetroot	3 tomatoes

*gammon or bacon chops are ideal

1 Dice the bacon, celery and apples.
2 Grate carrot.
3 Shred the cucumber and beetroot.
4 Mix the bacon, celery, carrot, apples and capers together.
5 Toss in mayonnaise.
6 Pile on to the lettuce and decorate with the eggs, tomatoes, cucumber and beetroot.

Cucumber boats

no cooking

you will need:

1 long straight	seasoning
cucumber	lemon juice

for filling:

flaked salmon,	minced or chopped
green peas and	cooked meat, very
mayonnaise, **or**	little chopped onion,
chopped hard-boiled	tomato sauce or
eggs, mayonnaise,	mayonnaise
and tomato, **or**	lettuce

1 Peel cucumber and cut into 1 or 2-inch lengths, cut across the centre to give 'boat shape'.
2 Scoop out centre pulp of cucumber and chop finely.
3 Season the boat-shaped shell and sprinkle with lemon juice.
4 Mix ingredients for filling together, pile into boat shapes.
5 Serve with crisp lettuce.

Cucumber salad

Finely slice 4 oz. cheese and 2 oz. shelled walnuts or put into electric slicer. Cover with lemon juice or vinegar and seasoning or make a

sour sweet dressing by blending 2 tablespoons oil, 1 tablespoon white vinegar or lemon juice, $\frac{1}{2}$ teaspoon sugar, seasoning. Pour this dressing over the cucumber and leave to stand for about 30 minutes before using.
Garnish with chopped dill or parsley.

Crab salad

no cooking

you will need:

1 can crab	2 hard-boiled eggs
1 lettuce	mayonnaise (see page
salt	57)
pepper	paprika

1 Flake the crab meat into a bed of crisp lettuce leaves.
2 Add salt and pepper.
3 Sieve yolks of eggs and sprinkle over crab meat.
4 Chop egg whites and sprinkle round meat.
5 Add $\frac{1}{2}$ teaspoon mayonnaise to each portion and a dash of paprika.

Herring salad

no cooking

you will need:

2 Bismark or rollmop or cooked herrings	8 oz. new potatoes, cooked
	1 beetroot, diced
	2 apples, diced

for dressing:

1 small onion, chopped	seasoning
	little vinegar
1 tablespoon salad oil	1 tablespoon cream or evaporated milk

1 Dice fish, vegetables and apples.
2 Mix all the ingredients for dressing and toss fish and vegetables in this.

Potato salad

cooking time: 25 minutes

you will need:

4 oz. celery	$\frac{1}{8}$ pint vinegar
4 oz. green peppers	$\frac{1}{4}$ pint hot water
6 small new potatoes	$\frac{1}{2}$ teaspoon salt
3 strips bacon, chopped small	2 oz. sugar
1 tablespoon flour	1 small onion, minced
	1 hard-boiled egg

1 Chop celery and peppers into small pieces.
2 Boil potatoes in jackets until nearly soft.
3 Peel while hot.
4 Fry chopped bacon until crisp and remove from pan.
5 Blend flour in bacon fat until smooth.

6 Add vinegar, water, salt and sugar.
7 Bring to boiling point and simmer for 5 minutes.
8 Place potatoes, onion, celery and green peppers in bowl.
9 Pour hot mixture over and mix lightly.
10 Turn into serving dish and top with bacon and sliced egg. Serve very cold.

Spring coleslaw

no cooking

you will need:

1 small cabbage	2–3 carrots
little mustard	4 oz. cheese
mayonnaise (see page 57)	2 oz. sultanas
	apple wedges, to garnish
2–3 eating apples	

1 Remove any tough outer leaves from cabbage.
2 Shred very finely.
3 Blend a little made mustard into mayonnaise.
4 Add to cabbage, together with grated apple, carrots and cheese and sultanas.
5 Pile into salad bowl.
6 Just before serving, garnish with wedges of apple.

Sunset salad

no cooking

you will need:

12 oz. cooked potatoes	seasoning
2 oz. raw carrot, grated	mayonnaise (see page 57)
1 tablespoon parsley, chopped	lettuce

1 Mash the potatoes and add carrot, parsley and seasoning.
2 Add a good tablespoon mayonnaise.
3 Mix well and then with your fingers form into small balls.
4 Put these on a bed of lettuce and pour extra mayonnaise over each of the balls.

Peach cheese salad

no cooking

you will need:

lettuce	cottage cheese, chive-flavoured or cottage cheese chopped chives
peaches, halved	

1 Arrange lettuce on a serving plate.
2 Pile peaches and chive-flavoured cottage cheese on top.

Stuffed tomato salads

Tomato cases make the basis of a number of easy and delicious salads, which may be served as a light main dish or as an hors-d'oeuvre. No cooking is required.

Tomato anchovy salad

1 Cut the tops off large firm tomatoes, turn upside down and allow to drain, having removed the centre pulp.
2 Chop this pulp and mix with chopped canned anchovies, hard-boiled egg and cress.
3 Pile back into tomato cases and serve on bed of lettuce.

Tomato beetroot salad

1 Cut the tops off large firm tomatoes, scoop out the centre pulp.
2 Allow the cases to drain for a while, then season lightly.
3 Mix the chopped centre pulp with diced beetroot and chopped hard-boiled egg white, then blend with mayonnaise (see page 57) or oil and vinegar.
4 Put back into the tomato cases and top with the chopped hard-boiled egg yolk.
5 Serve on a bed of watercress.

Tomato carrot salad

1 Cut the tops off large firm tomatoes and scoop out the centre pulp.
2 Allow the cases to drain and season well.
3 Mix the chopped pulp with grated raw carrot, chopped parsley, grated cheese, seasoning.
4 Pile back into tomato cases and top with chopped parsley.

Devilled tomato salad

1 Cut the tops off large firm tomatoes and scoop out the centre pulp.
2 Allow cases to drain and season with salt, pepper and a sprinkling of curry powder.

3 Chop the centre pulp and blend with seasoning, curry powder, little chutney and a few drops chilli or Worcestershire sauce.
4 Stir in cooked drained rice, and either chopped ham, hard-boiled eggs or flaked fish.
5 Pile back into tomato cases and top with mayonnaise, flavoured with a little curry powder.

Tomato egg salad

1 Cut the tops off large tomatoes and scoop out the centre pulp.
2 Allow the cases to drain and season lightly.
3 Chop the centre pulp, and the slices cut from the top, and fry gently in hot butter. Add beaten eggs, seasoning, chopped parsley and scramble lightly.
4 Blend in chopped chives or parsley and a little mayonnaise when the mixture is cool.
5 Fill the cases with this mixture and serve on a bed of green salad.

Tomato fish salad

1 Cut the tops off large tomatoes and scoop out the centre pulp.
2 If garlic is liked, rub the insides of the cases with a cut clove of garlic.
3 Chop the centre pulp and blend with flaked cooked white fish, diced cucumber, chopped watercress and lemon juice. Season well.
4 Pile back into tomato cases and garnish with sliced cucumber.

Tomato salad Indienne

1 Cut the tops off large tomatoes and scoop out the centre pulp.
2 Allow the cases to drain and season lightly, adding a squeeze of lemon juice.
3 Chop the pulp and fry the chopped 'lids' and pulp with finely-chopped onion in a little hot oil or butter.
4 Add little curry powder, cooked rice, chopped green pepper and blend thoroughly.
5 When cold, pile into tomato cases.

Winter salad

no cooking

you will need:

1 young cabbage	2 hard-boiled eggs
seasoning	beetroot
celery	2 carrots
2 sweet apples	

1 Discard the outer leaves of the cabbage and shred the heart very finely.
2 Season well and place into a salad bowl with the diced celery and thinly sliced apple.
3 Decorate with rings of hard-boiled egg, diced beetroot and grated carrot.

Classic mayonnaise

no cooking

you will need:

1 egg yolk	$\frac{1}{8}$–$\frac{1}{4}$ pint olive oil
good pinch salt, pepper and mustard	1 dessertspoon vinegar
	1 dessertspoon warm water

1 Put the egg yolk and seasonings into a basin.
2 Gradually beat in the oil, drop by drop, stirring all the time until the mixture is thick.
3 When it becomes creamy, stop adding oil for too much will make the mixture curdle.*
4 Beat in the vinegar gradually, then the warm water.
5 Use when fresh.

*if this does happen, break another egg into a bowl and add the curdled mixture drop by drop, beating hard.

Family mayonnaise

cooking time: 15 minutes

you will need:

3 tablespoons flour	1 tablespoon sugar
1 teaspoon dry mustard	1 egg
few grains cayenne or pepper	$\frac{1}{2}$ pint water
1 teaspoon salt	4 tablespoons vinegar
	3 tablespoons olive oil

1 Blend the flour, mustard, sugar and seasoning to make a paste with the egg.
2 Stir in the water gradually.
3 Add the vinegar and cook over boiling water until thick.
4 Allow to cook for a further 5 minutes.
5 Cool and beat in the oil.

Evaporated milk mayonnaise

no cooking

you will need:

1 6-oz. can evaporated milk	salt
$\frac{1}{4}$ pint olive oil	pepper
$\frac{1}{4}$ pint vinegar **or** lemon juice	about $\frac{1}{2}$ teaspoon castor sugar

1 Pour the milk into a bowl and whisk in the oil gradually.
2 Add the vinegar or lemon juice.
3 Season to taste with salt, pepper and sugar.

Tuna coleslaw salad

no cooking

you will need:

1 7-oz. can tuna	salt
6 oz. celery, finely chopped	pepper
1 tablespoon horseradish sauce	1 small Savoy cabbage
3 tablespoons salad cream or mayonnaise (see left)	3 tablespoons grated carrot
	2 hard-boiled eggs
	2 tomatoes

1 Mix the chopped fish with the celery, horseradish sauce, salad cream and a sprinkling of salt and pepper.
2 Pile on to a bed of finely shredded cabbage mixed with the carrot.
3 Garnish with sliced egg and tomato wedges.

Variations

With other fruit and vegetables – add chopped apple, shallot, onion, sweet pepper (capsicum) or capers.

With tomato purée – the horseradish sauce can be omitted and extra mayonnaise used, or blend a little tomato purée with the mayonnaise.

With shrimps – omit celery and substitute 4–6 oz. canned or frozen shrimps.

Chicken coleslaw salad – use recipe for tuna coleslaw salad but use 8 oz. cooked diced chicken instead of tuna.

Ham coleslaw salad – use recipe for tuna coleslaw salad but use approximately 8 oz. cooked diced ham instead of tuna.

Maryland seafood salad

no cooking

you will need:

8 oz. lobster or crabmeat, fresh or canned	2 teaspoons anchovy essence
12 oz. cooked rice	¼ level teaspoon dry mustard
2 tablespoons French dressing (see page 60)	3 oz. celery, finely sliced
3 tablespoons mayonnaise (see page 57)	2 tablespoons parsley, chopped
1 small onion, finely chopped	crisp lettuce leaves
	2 hard-boiled eggs

1 Break the shellfish into bite-size pieces and combine with the rice and French dressing.
2 Cover and chill for 30 minutes.
3 Mix the mayonnaise with the onion, anchovy essence and mustard.
4 Add to the rice mixture with the celery and parsley.
5 Toss lightly together.
6 Pile into a dish lined with lettuce leaves and garnish with eggs, quartered lengthwise.

Chicken salad

no cooking

you will need:

approximately 12 oz. chicken meat, diced (have good mixture of light and dark chicken meat)	about 4 oz. celery or chicory, diced
	mayonnaise (see page 57)
	lettuce
	red pepper

1 Blend chicken meat, celery and mayonnaise together.
2 Arrange on a bed of lettuce and garnish with strips of red pepper.

Coleslaw

no cooking

you will need:

white crisp cabbage	lemon juice
few sultanas, if liked	salad dressing or mayonnaise (see page 57)

1 Shred the washed and dried cabbage very finely.
2 Put into a basin with the sultanas and lemon juice.
3 Toss in salad dressing and serve very cold.

Variations

Celery coleslaw – use recipe above, but add finely diced celery to the cabbage.

Celery and apple coleslaw – use recipe before, but add finely diced celery and chopped dessert apple to the cabbage. Use plenty of lemon juice to make sure the apple keeps a good colour.

Savoury coleslaw – use same recipe, but add chopped gherkins, capers, parsley to the cabbage, together with a small amount of chopped chives or spring onion. Toss in mayonnaise or salad dressing or well-seasoned oil and vinegar.

Rice and chicken salad

cooking time: 15 minutes

you will need:

8 oz. long grain rice	1–2 tablespoons vinegar*
1 pint water	salt and pepper
1 level teaspoon salt	1 heaped tablespoon currants or raisins
clove garlic (optional)	1 green pepper
4 tablespoons salad oil	2 large tomatoes
	12 oz. cooked chicken

*wine or tarragon for preference

1 Put the rice, water and salt into a saucepan and cook until rice is dry and fluffy.
2 Rub a salad bowl with the cut clove of garlic and in it mix together the oil, vinegar and seasonings.
3 Add the hot rice and currants and toss lightly with the dressing.
4 De-seed and very finely slice the green pepper.
5 De-seed and chop the tomatoes and cut the chicken into bite-size pieces.
6 Stir all into the salad, reserving a few pieces of pepper and tomato for garnishing the top of the salad.
7 Cover and set aside in a cool place for the flavours to blend.

Stuffed egg salad

no cooking

you will need:

4 hard-boiled eggs	seasoning
4 tomatoes	large lettuce leaves
4 teaspoons mayonnaise (see page 57) or sandwich spread	

1 Cut eggs across the centre lengthwise.
2 Remove yolks carefully and put these into a basin.
3 Skin the tomatoes, cut into slices and mix with yolks.

4 Add mayonnaise and seasoning and pound well.

5 Fill centres of eggs with this mixture, press tightly together and roll in lettuce leaves.

Egg and tomato salad

no cooking

you will need:

6 hard-boiled eggs	salt
4 tomatoes	pepper
mayonnaise (see page 57)	lettuce

1 Cut eggs in half lengthwise and remove yolks.

2 Skin tomatoes and pound them down in a basin.

3 Add the mayonnaise, yolks, salt and pepper to taste.

4 Fill whites of egg with mixture and serve on very crisp lettuce leaves.

Stuffed tomatoes

no cooking

you will need:

4 even-sized tomatoes	1 dessertspoon cucumber, chopped
2 hard-boiled eggs, chopped	1 tablespoon salad cream

1 Cut 'lids' off tomatoes and remove centres.

2 Mix eggs, cucumber and salad cream together, fill each tomato with the mixture.

3 Replace lids.

4 Serve with salad.

Mayonnaise (without eggs)

no cooking

you will need:

1 level teaspoon mustard	1 small can evaporated milk
1 teaspoon sugar	$\frac{1}{2}$ pint olive oil
$\frac{1}{2}$ teaspoon salt	2–3 tablespoons wine vinegar
pinch pepper	

1 Put the mustard into a bowl with sugar, salt and a large pinch pepper.

2 Add the evaporated milk.

3 Mix and beat in by degrees the olive oil.

4 Add the vinegar, when the mixture will thicken.

5 Season to taste.

Economical salad dressing

no cooking

you will need:

1 small can full cream condensed milk	$\frac{1}{4}$ pint vinegar
$\frac{1}{2}$ teaspoon salt	1 teaspoon dry mustard

1 Mix all the ingredients and beat well.

2 Chill or cool before serving.

Mayonnaise in-a-blender

blender speed: high then low

you will need for 6–8 servings:

2 egg yolks	1 level teaspoon dry mustard
$\frac{1}{4}$ level teaspoon pepper	pinch sugar
1 level teaspoon salt	2–4 tablespoons vinegar
$\frac{1}{4}$ level teaspoon paprika	up to $\frac{1}{2}$ pint oil

1 See the blender goblet is dry and cool before you begin.

2 Place egg yolks in goblet, add seasonings and sugar.

3 Add half the vinegar. Switch on to a high speed for about 15 seconds.

4 If using a blender with a cap in the lid, remove this. If not, tilt the lid so oil may be added without splashing.

5 Add oil very steadily on a fairly low speed. Continue adding oil until the mayonnaise is as thick as you like. The more oil that is added, providing it is not put in too quickly, the thicker the mayonnaise will be.

6 Add the rest of the vinegar at the end.

Note

A tablespoon of very hot water put in at the end gives you a very creamy mayonnaise.

Variation

Green mayonnaise – make mayonnaise above. Add a sprig of parsley, 1 or 2 leaves of chives, 1 or 2 leaves of sage and a tiny sprig of mint. Put into the blender goblet with mayonnaise, switch on until the herbs are very finely chopped.

French dressing

no cooking

you will need:

1 dessertspoon vinegar	salt
1 tablespoon salad oil	pepper
pinch sugar	1 tablespoon parsley, finely chopped or chives

Mix all the ingredients together in a basin.

Sweet French dressing

no cooking

you will need:

1 teaspoon vinegar	3 dessertspoons olive oil
1 teaspoon salt	1 dessertspoon white wine **or** vinegar **or** 1½ dessertspoons lemon juice
pinch paprika	
1–2 teaspoons sugar	

Place all the ingredients in a screw-top jar and shake well together. Pour the dressing over the salad just before serving.

Food for Your Unexpected Guest

It is a warm tribute to your home if your friends feel they can pop in and see you on the spur of the moment, or with very little notice. The snacks in this section have been chosen so that they can be adjusted to give slightly more luxury when unexpected guests arrive.

It is wise to keep one or two cans of vegetables including the more unusual red and green peppers, corn, etc., in the cupboard because by adding these to quite ordinary ingredients a snack can become a rather special dish.

To boil rice easily

Use 1 measure of rice – i.e. cup or measure	Use 2 measures of water – exactly the same measure used for measuring rice salt to taste

1 Put the water, rice and salt into a saucepan.
2 Bring to the boil, stir then cover with a tightly fitting lid and lower heat.
3 Simmer gently for approximately 15 minutes, when all the water will be absorbed – the rice will not need rinsing.

Salmon crisp

cooking time: 5 minutes

you will need:

4 slices bread	1 small can salmon
little butter	2 gherkins

for topping:

2 tablespoons breadcrumbs	few drops anchovy sauce or anchovy essence
2 tablespoons cheese, grated	1 tablespoon milk

1 Toast and butter the bread.
2 Spread with the mashed salmon and chopped gherkins.
3 Blend the crumbs, cheese, anchovy sauce and milk and spread over the top of the salmon.
4 Put under a hot grill for 2 or 3 minutes until crisp.

For the unexpected guest – make even more interesting with fans of gherkins on crisp lettuce, or more substantial by topping with poached eggs.

Salmon shell casserole

cooking time: 50 minutes–1 hour

you will need:

3 oz. shell or elbow macaroni	lemon juice
½ pint cheese sauce (see page 83)	breadcrumbs
1 medium sized can red or pink salmon	butter or margarine
	parsley

1 Cook macaroni in boiling salted water until tender.
2 Stir into sauce with flaked salmon, add squeeze lemon juice.
3 Put into casserole, top with crumbs and small knobs butter or margarine.
4 Cook in a moderate oven for 30 minutes (375°F. – Gas Mark 4). Garnish with parsley.

For the unexpected guest – serve with crisp lettuce, or top with canned asparagus tips.

Salmon horseradish shells

no cooking

you will need:

lettuce
cooked or canned
  salmon

cucumber, diced
horseradish cream

for garnish:

cucumber, sliced

hard-boiled egg

1 Arrange rather large cup-shaped pieces of lettuce on the serving dish.
2 Flake the salmon and put on to the lettuce leaves, together with the diced cucumber.
3 Top with the horseradish cream – or if preferred use equal quantities of horseradish cream and mayonnaise (see page 57).
4 Garnish with the sliced cucumber and egg.

For the unexpected guest – top the hard-boiled eggs with anchovy fillets to make the mixture more sustaining, and garnish with asparagus tips.

Speedy casserole

cooking time: 30 minutes

you will need:

1 can condensed
  cream of mushroom
  soup
¼ pint yoghourt
1 large can salmon,
  flaked, or 8 oz.
  cooked chicken
  pieces

1 can sweet corn
2 hard-boiled eggs,
  chopped
¼ teaspoon dry
  mustard
salt .
pepper

1 Blend soup with yoghourt and liquid from salmon, or chicken stock.
2 Combine with sweet corn (drained), flaked salmon or chicken, eggs and seasoning.
3 Pour into greased casserole and bake in a moderate oven (375°F. – Gas Mark 4) for 25–30 minutes.

Variation

With evaporated milk – when yoghourt is not available, use evaporated milk and a little lemon juice.

For the unexpected guest – top with asparagus tips, or serve with a crisp mixed salad.

Tuna Espagnole

cooking time: 25 minutes

you will need:

2 7-oz. cans tuna fish
2 tablespoons corn
  oil
1 large onion, sliced
1 green pepper,
  chopped

½ pint tomato sauce*
  (see page 84)
1 lb. creamed potatoes
½ oz. cornflakes,
  crushed
1 oz. grated cheese

*or use tomato sauce mix, or soup

1 Flake the fish.
2 Heat the corn oil and sauté the onion and pepper until soft.
3 Add the fish, onion and pepper. Add tomato sauce and mix well together.
4 Put into a fireproof dish and cover with the mashed potatoes.
5 Sprinkle with the cornflakes and cheese.
6 Bake for 10–15 minutes in a hot oven (425°F. – Gas Mark 6).

For the unexpected guest – serve with baked tomatoes and canned corn.

Paella

cooking time: 30 minutes

you will need:

4 joints cooked
  chicken
1 onion
1 clove garlic
  (optional)
2 tablespoons
  olive oil
2 pints water
3 tomatoes
4 oz. rice
2 chicken bouillon
  cubes

little saffron, if
  possible
1 can lobster
4 Dublin Bay prawns
  or 8–10 smaller
  prawns, shelled
6–8 mussels
8 oz. cooked or
  frozen peas
¼ can pimento or red
  pepper

1 Cut up chicken, onion and garlic and fry in the oil until golden.
2 Add half water and simmer for 15 minutes.
3 Add tomatoes, skinned and chopped.
4 Add rice and remaining water and bouillon cubes.
5 Simmer for 5 minutes, stir in saffron.
6 Arrange the lobster pieces, prawns, mussels and peas attractively with the pimento.
7 Continue cooking until rice is cooked and has absorbed most of the liquid.

For the unexpected guest – no need to 'dress up' this dish, it is sufficiently exciting by itself. Just serve with green salad.

Chilli con corn

cooking time: 1–1¾ hours

you will need:

2 oz. margarine or butter	8 oz. tomatoes (fresh or canned)
1 large onion	¼ pint water (little less with canned tomatoes)
2 sticks celery	
2 cloves garlic	
12 oz.–1 lb. beef, minced or diced	½ teaspoon salt
1 tablespoon flour	1 can sweet corn and peppers
1 tablespoon chilli powder*	

*this is very hot, and in consequence very much a matter of personal taste, so add only a teaspoon of chilli powder the first time you make the dish, taste during cooking and add the rest as desired

1 Heat the margarine in a saucepan.
2 Chop the onion and celery and crush the cloves of garlic.
3 Cook in the margarine until just tender.
4 Add the meat and brown for a few minutes. If using minced meat, take care to break into small pieces.
5 Stir in the flour and chilli powder.
6 Gradually add the tomatoes, water and salt.
7 Bring to the boil, stir until thickened slightly.
8 Lower the heat and cover the pan.
9 Cook gently for approximately 50 minutes if using minced beef, or 1½ hours if using diced beef.
10 Stir half way during the cooking and add a little more water if necessary.
11 The corn and peppers may either be put into the mixture 5 minutes before serving, or heated separately and piled into the centre of the serving dish or dishes.

For the unexpected guest – this is another satisfying and unusual dish that just needs a green salad.

Risotto

cooking time: 40 minutes

you will need:

4 oz. cooked chicken	¼ pint chicken stock or water with bouillon cube
2 oz. cooked ham	
2 tomatoes	
1 oz. margarine	salt
1 onion, finely chopped	ground black pepper
1 clove garlic, crushed	1 medium can peas or cooked peas
6 oz. rice	Parmesan cheese

1 Cut chicken and ham into strips.

2 Skin, seed and cut tomatoes into strips.
3 Melt the margarine in a frying pan.
4 Fry the onion and garlic lightly.
5 Add the rice and cook until all the fat is absorbed.
6 Stir in the stock and simmer gently for about 30 minutes until the rice is just cooked.
7 Adjust seasoning with salt and freshly ground black pepper.
8 Add the chicken, ham, tomato and drained peas.
9 Heat through.
10 Serve immediately, accompanied by grated Parmesan cheese.

For the unexpected guest – add chopped canned peppers if liked and serve with a crisp green salad. This is an ideal dish as it keeps warm over a low heat without spoiling.

Bacon macaroni and cheese

cooking time: 15 minutes

you will need:

4 oz. quick cooking elbow macaroni	2–3 rashers streaky bacon
1 can condensed tomato soup	small onion, if wished
	seasoning
about ¼ pint milk	1 slice bread
4–6 oz. grated cheese	knob of butter
	parsley

1 Put the macaroni into boiling salted water and cook rapidly for 7 minutes.
2 To make the sauce, heat the soup and enough milk to give coating consistency together.
3 Add most of the cheese.
4 While the macaroni is cooking, fry the chopped bacon and chopped onion, if using this, and add to the tomato sauce. Add seasoning.
5 Dice the slice of bread, add a knob of butter to any bacon fat in the pan.
6 Cook the bread until golden brown.
7 Strain the macaroni and mix with the tomato mixture.
8 Pour into a casserole and top with the cubes of bread and the rest of the cheese.
9 Garnish with parsley.

Variation

Heating in the oven – this dish can be heated through in the oven, allowing about 20 minutes. Since the macaroni will absorb more liquid this way, use nearly ½ pint milk.

For the unexpected guest – serve with green salad and canned or cooked mushrooms.

Sweet corn and ham casserole

cooking time: 20–25 minutes

you will need:

1 oz. butter	2 oz. grated cheese
1 oz. cornflour	1 can corn
1 chicken stock cube	4 oz. cooked ham, diced
½ pint milk	little red pepper, chopped
¼ pint water	
2 oz. fresh white breadcrumbs	

1 Melt the butter.
2 Add the cornflour and stock cube and cook for 1 minute.
3 Add the liquid and bring to the boil, stirring all the time.
4 Cook for a further 1 minute and remove from the heat.
5 Add most of the breadcrumbs and cheese (reserve the remainder for sprinkling on top) and add the remaining ingredients.
6 Pour into a well-greased casserole, sprinkle the remaining breadcrumbs and cheese on top.
7 Bake in a moderate oven (375°F. – Gas Mark 4) for 15 minutes.
8 Brown under grill before serving, if necessary.

For the unexpected guest – serve with baked or grilled tomatoes and a green salad.

Bacon pizza — English style

cooking time: 1¼ hours

you will need:

for dough:

8 oz. plain flour	¼ pint warm milk
1 teaspoon salt	2 eggs
½ oz. yeast	2 oz. softened butter
1 teaspoon sugar	olive oil

for topping:

1 small can tomato purée	6–8 rashers streaky or back bacon
8 slices processed or Cheddar cheese	3–4 stuffed olives

1 Sieve and warm the flour and salt.
2 Cream together yeast and sugar, add the milk and beaten eggs.
3 Make a well in the flour, add the liquid, then add the softened butter and beat well.
4 Cover and leave to rise for 40 minutes.

5 Spread the dough on to a well-oiled square baking tin and cover and leave to prove for 10 minutes, then bake in a moderate oven for 20–30 minutes.
6 When the pizza is required, spread with tomato purée.
7 Then cover with slices of cheese and rashers of bacon (rind removed) and place under a hot grill or in the oven until the cheese has melted and the bacon cooked, about 10 minutes.
8 Decorate with sliced olives and serve.
9 If a thin crisp pizza is preferred, divide the dough into two, cook both rounds and reheat as necessary.

For the unexpected guest – nothing need be added to this interesting savoury dish, except perhaps crisp watercress and lettuce.

Gnocchi

cooking time: 15–25 minutes

you will need:

½ pint water	4 oz. grated cheese
4 oz. semolina seasoning	2 teaspoons onion, grated (optional)
2 oz. butter or margarine	

1 Bring the water to the boil.
2 Whisk on the semolina.
3 Cook for 10 minutes, stirring well for the mixture is very thick.
4 Add the seasoning and butter or margarine and ¾ of the cheese and the onion.
5 Turn the paste on to a plate or board.
6 Allow to cool slightly, then roll out thinly.
7 Cup into shapes, press the grated cheese on top.
8 Either bake in a hot oven or crisp under a hot grill.
9 Serve with a salad, or with cheese sauce (see page 83).

For the unexpected guest – serve with the cheese sauce or cheese flavoured mayonnaise (i.e. add a little crumbled blue cheese or grated cheese to mayonnaise). Garnish the gnocchi with rings of tomato and olives.

Bacon Imperial

cooking time: 1 hour

you will need:

12 rashers streaky
  or back bacon

for mushroom stuffing:

1 tablespoon onion, finely chopped	3 oz. breadcrumbs
2 oz. margarine or butter	2 teaspoons parsley, finely chopped
6 oz. mushrooms (use mushroom stalks only if wished)	1 egg seasoning

for filling the ring:

(a) hard-boiled eggs in creamed sauce	(b) braised kidneys
	(c) mixed vegetables

1 Remove the rind from the bacon and if the rashers are very long cut each rasher in half.
2 Make the stuffing by frying the onion in the hot margarine, adding the chopped mushrooms and the rest of the ingredients.
3 Put a little of this on each rasher of bacon and roll firmly.
4 When all the rashers of bacon are filled and rolled, arrange in a small ring mould – packing them tightly.
5 Bake for approximately 45 minutes in the centre of a moderately hot oven (400°F. – Gas Mark 5) until the bacon is crisp and golden brown.
6 Turn out carefully and fill with the kidney, egg or vegetable mixture.
7 Serve with baked tomatoes, green salad and piped potatoes.

(a) To make egg in creamed sauce filling – make ½ pint white sauce, add 1 or 2 tablespoons cream and 4 or 5 hard-boiled eggs, cut into neat slices. Garnish with parsley sprigs.

(b) To make kidney filling – divide 4 or 5 lamb's kidneys into quarters, dust well with seasoned flour. Fry gently in 2 oz. butter, then gradually stir in ¼ pint of stock. Simmer gently until the kidneys are tender and the sauce thickened, season well, then add ⅛ pint of Madeira, sherry or port wine. Garnish with sliced hard-boiled egg.

(c) To make vegetable filling – dice and cook as colourful a selection of vegetables as possible. Toss in plenty of melted butter or margarine and garnish with parsley.

For the unexpected guest – serve with canned or frozen creamed spinach (i.e. cooked spinach to which is added a little top of the milk and butter) and/or baked tomatoes and crusty bread.

Mushroom and tomato pasta

cooking time: 40 minutes

you will need:

1 15-oz. can tomato juice	1 level teaspoon Worcestershire sauce
water	seasoning
½ level teaspoon celery salt	5 oz. fine semolina
1 level teaspoon onion salt	4 oz. mushrooms
1 level teaspoon sugar	1 oz. butter
	1 egg
	cheese sauce (see page 83)
	cheese

1 Make up tomato juice to 1 pint with water.
2 Add seasonings. Heat gently.
3 Stir in semolina and cook, stirring, till mixture comes to the boil and thickens (about 3 to 4 minutes) over a very low heat.
4 Fry chopped mushrooms.
5 Beat in egg to semolina mixture and add mushrooms.
6 Cook for a further 2 minutes.
7 Transfer mixture to well-oiled, shallow tin.
8 Leave till firm.
9 Cut into small diamonds, triangles or circles and arrange pasta attractively in a heatproof dish.
10 Coat with cheese sauce (or sour cream).
11 Sprinkle with about 1 oz. grated cheese.
12 Re-heat and brown in moderate oven at (375°F. – Gas Mark 4) for 25 to 30 minutes.

Rice and cheese croquettes

cooking time: 25 minutes

you will need:

¼ pint milk or stock	1 tomato
2 oz. rice	2 oz. grated cheese
1 small onion	1 egg
salt	crisp breadcrumbs
cayenne pepper	fat for frying
dry mustard	2 teaspoons Parmesan cheese (optional)

1 Bring milk or stock to boil, shake in rice.
2 Add whole onion and seasoning.
3 Cook steadily for about 15 minutes until rice is quite soft.

4 Towards end of cooking time, you must stir once or twice to stop rice from burning.

5 Remove the onion, then add skinned sliced tomato and grated cheese to the rice, stirring well.

6 Let mixture cool, taste and add additional seasoning as desired.

7 Form into shape of croquettes and brush lightly with beaten egg or milk.

8 Coat with breadcrumbs and fry until crisp and brown.

9 Drain well and sprinkle with Parmesan cheese.

Note

These make an equally good dish to serve hot at home with grilled tomatoes and mushrooms, or to carry on a picnic.

For the unexpected guest – to make a complete dish, just garnish well and serve attractively.

Curried hard-boiled eggs

cooking time: 45 minutes

you will need:

for sauce:

1 oz. butter	1 teaspoon chutney
1 small onion	few sultanas
1 small piece apple	2 teaspoons coconut
1–2 teaspoons	seasoning
curry powder	6–8 hard-boiled eggs
1 teaspoon flour	3–4 oz. cooked
½ pint white stock	Patna rice

1 Make the sauce by frying the onion and apple in the butter.

2 Work in the curry powder, flour and then add the stock.

3 Bring to the boil and cook until smooth, then add the flavourings and simmer the sauce for about ½ hour.

4 Add the halved eggs, warm and serve in a border of rice.

5 Serve sliced tomatoes, grated carrots, sliced gherkins in dishes with the egg curry and, of course, a dish of chutney.

Variation

Creamed curry – make the hard-boiled egg curry, but instead of using stock use nearly ⅓ pint milk and ⅛ pint cream in the sauce. Cooking time: 25–30 minutes.
Garnish with wedges of lemon.

For the unexpected guest – add a few extra 'side dishes' e.g. sliced cucumber, banana, chopped apple, coconut, etc.

Southern casserole

cooking time: 35 minutes

you will need:

8 small cocktail	1 oz. butter
sausages	seasoning
3 oz. elbow	6–8 oz. processed
spaghetti	cheese
1 can creamed corn	
on the cob	

1 Grill, fry or bake the sausages. Keep hot.

2 Meanwhile cook the spaghetti until tender.

3 Strain and mix with the creamed corn on the cob and butter.

4 Season well.

5 Put a layer at the bottom of a casserole, cover with a layer of processed cheese, then a layer of corn on the cob mixture.

6 Top with a thick layer of cheese.

7 Cook for 15 minutes in moderately hot oven (400–425°F. – Gas Mark 5–6) until cheese melts.

8 Arrange sausages on top.

Egg and savoury rice

no cooking

you will need:

3 oz. Patna rice,	1 dessertspoon
cooked	sultanas
4 hard-boiled eggs	3 dessertspoons salad
2 oz. peeled	cream
shrimps	½ teaspoon lemon
1 teaspoon capers,	juice
chopped	
¼ bunch watercress,	
chopped	

for garnish:

2 tomatoes	lettuce

1 Mix cold rice with 3 chopped hard-boiled eggs and other dry ingredients.

2 Bind with salad cream and lemon juice.

3 Place in shallow dish and garnish with sliced egg, tomato and lettuce.

For the unexpected guest – make the salad a little more exciting and filling by adding asparagus tips, canned sweet corn, canned chopped peppers.

Devilled eggs, Spanish style (hot)

cooking time: 25–30 minutes

you will need:

6 hard-boiled eggs	2 oz. celery, finely
little milk	chopped (optional)
Worcestershire	1 oz. flour
sauce	1 teaspoon sugar
made mustard	salt and pepper
2 oz. butter	1 lb. tomatoes
1 small onion,	breadcrumbs
chopped	

1 Cut eggs in halves, lengthwise, and remove yolks.
2 Press yolks through a sieve.
3 Moisten them with a little milk and flavour with Worcestershire sauce and mustard.
4 Refill whites with this mixture.
5 Melt butter over low heat, add onion and celery and cook until onion is transparent.
6 Blend in flour, sugar and seasonings.
7 Heat the skinned, roughly chopped tomatoes and gradually add these to the butter and flour mixture, stirring constantly.
8 Cook until thickened.
9 Pour mixture into a shallow baking dish.
10 Arrange devilled eggs in the sauce, top with crumbs.
11 Place in a hot oven until sauce is bubbly round the edges (10–15 minutes).
12 Serve with cooked rice, spaghetti, noodles, or on toast.

For the unexpected guest – serve with thin slices of cucumber, tomato and cocktail onions.

Eggs au gratin

cooking time: 25–30 minutes

you will need:

6 hard-boiled eggs	4 oz. mushrooms
1 oz. butter	parsley
½ pint white sauce	4 oz. bacon or ham
(see page 83)	salt and pepper

1 Slice eggs fairly thickly.
2 Well cover the bottom of a buttered pie dish with white sauce.
3 Arrange a layer of eggs on this.
4 Cover with a layer of thinly sliced mushrooms, chopped parsley and finely chopped bacon or ham.
5 Sprinkle with pepper and salt.

6 Repeat the layers until the dish is full, ending with white sauce.
7 Dot the top with knobs of butter.
8 Bake in a hot oven until browned.
9 Serve at once.

Variation

With rice – add a little cooked rice to the dish, in which case use ¾ pint sauce. The mushrooms can be fried in a little butter first to give a richer texture.

For the unexpected guest – serve with baked tomatoes and canned corn.

Egg and ham casserole

cooking time: 25–30 minutes

you will need:

4 hard-boiled eggs	½ pint white sauce
4 oz. ham, chopped	(see page 83)
2 oz. grated	breadcrumbs
cheese (preferably	cooked diced carrots
Parmesan)	few green peas

1 Halve the eggs and put them, cut side downwards, into a casserole.
2 Add the chopped ham and half the cheese to the sauce.
3 Pour over the eggs.
4 Add rest of the cheese and a few breadcrumbs.
5 Cook for approximately 20 minutes in a hot oven until crisp and golden brown on top.
6 Garnish with carrots and peas.

For the unexpected guest – this is a complete dish and only needs a salad to serve with it. The casserole looks more interesting if a border of triangles of toast or fried bread is arranged round the edge.

Hard-boiled egg and sausage galantine

cooking time: 30–45 minutes

you will need:

8 oz. sausage meat	4 tablespoons milk
2 dessertspoons	2 hard-boiled eggs
onion, chopped	breadcrumbs

1 Mix all the ingredients, except the eggs and breadcrumbs with the sausage meat.

2 Press out into an oblong shape, then put the eggs in the middle, or make two oblong shapes putting an egg in each.

3 Roll out the sausage mixture round the egg.

4 Bake on a greased tin for 30 minutes in a moderately hot oven (425°F. – Gas Mark 5), or steam for 45 minutes.

5 When cooked, roll in crumbs and allow to cool.

6 Cut in slices and pack between lettuce leaves and keep moist, if taking on a picnic.

For the unexpected guest – serve slices on a bed of green salad, garnish with canned corn and/or peas, sliced tomatoes, sliced gherkins or cucumber. To make a more substantial meal use canned beans topped with chopped parsley or chives.

Golden ring

cooking time: 10 minutes

you will need:

5 hard-boiled eggs	1 pint tomato juice
1 small packet frozen peas	seasoning lettuce
½ oz. powdered gelatine	little cream cheese if wished

1 Shell and cut the eggs into halves across the centre.

2 Cook and drain peas.

3 Dissolve the gelatine in the hot tomato juice.

4 Pour little of this into a ring mould, brushed with little olive oil.

5 When lightly set arrange the halved eggs, cut side downwards on to the jelly, and the peas to form an attractive pattern.

6 Spoon over a very little of the tomato gelatine mixture.

7 When set add rest of tomato liquid.

8 Turn out when quite firm on to a bed of lettuce and decorate with cream cheese.

9 In summer, garnish with thinly sliced cucumber and mixed fresh vegetables, served in mayonnaise. In winter, grated carrot, grated cheese, chopped gherkins or olives make a good filling for the centre of the ring.

For the unexpected guest – this is gay enough for entertaining but make more substantial by including more salad vegetables.

Harlequin corn

cooking time: 15–20 minutes

you will need:

2 corn on the cob* seasoning	1 onion or 6 spring onions
½ red pepper (capsicum)	4 tomatoes
	1 carrot, grated
½ green pepper (capsicum)	2 oz. butter

*canned or frozen corn can be used

1 Cook corn on the cob until just tender; remember **not** to add salt until about end of cooking time as this helps to make it tender.

2 Strip corn from cob.

3 Chop all vegetables and fry with carrot in hot butter.

4 Add corn.

5 Serve with crisp bacon rolls, or roast or creamed chicken, or plenty of grated cheese.

For the unexpected guest – serve with crisp salad and fresh bread.

Potato and vegetable gâteau

cooking time: 1¼–1½ hours

you will need:

1¼ lb. new potatoes	pinch mixed herbs
4 onions	seasoning
4 tomatoes	½ pint white or
3 oz. margarine	cheese sauce (see
2 carrots, grated	page 83)

1 Slice potatoes very thinly.

2 Fry thinly sliced onions and tomatoes in 2 oz. hot margarine.

3 Add grated carrot, herbs, seasoning.

4 Grease a round tin or oven casserole.

5 Put in ⅓ of the potatoes, season well and arrange neatly in a definite pattern.

6 Cover with half the sauce and half the onion and tomato mixture.

7 Put on another ⅓ of the potatoes and the rest of the sauce and mixture.

8 Finally, put on a layer of potatoes and remainder of margarine.

9 Cover tin with foil or lid.

10 Cook for approximately 1¼ hours in the centre of a moderate oven (350–375°F. – Gas Mark 3–4) until tender.

11 Remove lid for last 30 minutes.

For the unexpected guest – serve with baked tomatoes or green salad.

Prune and pepper kedgeree

cooking time: 15 minutes

you will need:

4 oz. unsalted
  butter
8 oz. fluffy boiled
  Patna rice
12 oz. cooked
  Finnan (smoked)
  haddock, flaked
1 red or green
  pepper, cooked and
  chopped

3 oz. prunes, stoned
  and chopped
4 oz. cooked peas,
  fresh or frozen
2 hard-boiled eggs,
  chopped
salt, pepper and lemon
  juice to taste
little lemon rind,
  grated

for garnish:

1 hard-boiled egg
6 prunes, stoned

lemon wedges

1 Melt the butter in a large pan.
2 Stir in the boiled rice.
3 Add flaked fish, chopped pepper, prunes and peas.
4 Mix well and add chopped hard-boiled egg.
5 Stir well, adding more butter if mixture is too dry.
6 Season well with salt, pepper, lemon juice and rind.
7 Pile upon hot dish.
8 For the garnish, separate white from egg yolk. Chop white and sieve yolk.
9 Arrange egg, prunes and lemon wedges round rice.

For the unexpected guest – this is a very colourful and satisfying dish, just serve surrounded with green salad, cooked vegetables, canned peas or asparagus and either sliced tomatoes or fried tomatoes.

Macaroni au gratin

cooking time: 45–50 minutes

you will need:

1 pint white stock
1 onion
2–3 cloves
small bunch herbs
8 oz. macaroni
seasoning

made mustard
4–6 oz. grated cheese
2 tablespoons
  breadcrumbs
little butter

1 Put the stock in a large saucepan with the onion stuck with the cloves and the herbs.
2 Bring to the boil and add the macaroni.
3 When tender, remove the onion and herbs and season well with salt and pepper and a little made mustard.

4 Grease a fireproof dish and put in alternate layers of macaroni and cheese, topping with cheese.
5 Cover with breadcrumbs and dot with butter and place in a hot oven (425°F. – Gas Mark 6) until nicely browned and sizzling hot.

For the unexpected guest – serve with mushrooms, bacon rolls and baked or grilled tomatoes.

Lasagna

cooking time: 1¼–1½ hours

you will need:

4 oz. lasagna
bacon and beef sauce
  (see below)
6 oz. Cheddar or
  Gruyère cheese,
  sliced

about 4 oz. cream
  cheese
little grated
  Parmesan cheese

for bacon and beef sauce:

2 oz. butter
1 onion
2 oz. mushrooms
1 carrot
4 oz. streaky
  bacon

½–¾ pint water or stock
  or 8 oz. fresh
  tomatoes and ½ pint
  stock
small tin concentrated
  tomato purée
4–6 oz. minced raw
  beef
seasoning

1 Cook the lasagna in plenty of boiling salted water until soft – this takes about 20 minutes. Other types of macaroni should be cooked according to directions on packet.
2 To make sauce, heat butter in pan and fry the chopped onion, chopped mushrooms and finely chopped carrot.
3 Add the diced bacon and fry for a few minutes further.
4 Put in the stock or water, tomato purée, meat, seasoning and bring to the boil.
5 Cook steadily until mixture thickens, the meat cooked.
6 When the lasagna is cooked, strain carefully from the water and allow to dry out for a while.
7 Cut into neat lengths.
8 Put a layer of lasagna, a layer of meat sauce, then a layer of thinly sliced Cheddar cheese, cream cheese and a sprinkling of Parmesan cheese.
9 Add another layer of lasagna, the rest of the meat sauce, more lasagna and a final layer of

the cheese, ending with sliced Cheddar cheese.

10 Put into a moderately hot oven for approximately 30 minutes until golden brown.
11 Serve with green vegetables or a crisp salad.

For the unexpected guest – this is such a complete dish that all it needs is a crisp mixed or green salad.

Harlequin rice

cooking time: 40–50 minutes

you will need:

2 onions, finely sliced	pinch salt
1 oz. dripping or fat	pinch pepper
1 large can tomatoes	few drops hot sauce (chilli or tabasco)
½ pint apple juice or stock	½ clove garlic, minced
	6 oz. rice, uncooked
	2 tablespoons olives

1 Brown onions in dripping or fat.
2 Add remaining ingredients.
3 Pour into shallow baking dish and cover.
4 Bake for 40–50 minutes in a very moderate oven (350°F. – Gas Mark 3) until rice is tender.
5 Twice during last 20 minutes of cooking, toss rice mixture lightly with a fork.
6 Serve with sausages, cheese or cold meat.

For the unexpected guest – serve with lots of grated cheese and/or Frankfurter sausages or grilled slices of luncheon meat.

Curry spaghetti platter

cooking time: 25–30 minutes

you will need:

6 oz. spaghetti

for sauce:

2 oz. butter or margarine	1 medium sized can tomatoes
little chopped onion	seasoning
1 teaspoon mustard	1 teaspoon Worcestershire sauce
2 teaspoons curry powder	
1 oz. flour	4 oz. ham, diced
	3 oz. Cheddar cheese

1 Put the spaghetti into boiling salted water.
2 Meanwhile, prepare the sauce. Heat butter and fry the onion.

3 Blend mustard, curry powder and flour and stir into the onion mixture.
4 Cook, stirring well for 2–3 minutes.
5 Add canned tomatoes.
6 Cook, stirring all the time, until a smooth thick sauce.
7 Season, and if too thick add a little water with the Worcestershire sauce.
8 Arrange the spaghetti on a long dish.
9 Add the diced ham and cheese to the sauce and pour over the spaghetti.

For the unexpected guest – serve with plenty of grated cheese and salad.

Spanish rice au gratin

cooking time: 40 minutes

you will need:

8 oz. long grain rice	1 lb. ripe tomatoes
1 pint water	2 tablespoons tomato ketchup
2 oz. butter	1 teaspoon Worcestershire sauce
6 oz. onion, chopped	salt and chilli powder to taste
4 oz. celery, chopped	little sugar
2 small green peppers	4 oz. grated cheese

1 Cook the rice in the water.
2 Meanwhile, melt the butter in a large frying pan.
3 Add the onion, celery and de-seeded and sliced peppers.
4 Cook gently until tender, stirring frequently.
5 Add the skinned and sliced tomatoes, ketchup, sauce, seasoning, and sugar to taste.
6 Stir in the cooked rice and simmer until thick.
7 Turn into a buttered casserole dish and sprinkle surface with cheese.
8 Place under a hot grill and cook until cheese melts to a golden brown.

For the unexpected guest – make a little more substantial by topping with bacon rashers and serve with canned or frozen vegetables, or salad.

Savouries Made with Pastry

These are ideal for picnics, buffet meals or for family suppers. The recipes for making the various kinds of pastry are given first.

Short crust pastry

you will need:

8 oz. flour	4 oz. fat
good pinch salt	cold water to mix

1 Sieve flour and salt.
2 Rub in fat until mixture looks like fine breadcrumbs.
3 Using first a knife and then the fingers to feel pastry, gradually add enough cold water to make dough into a rolling consistency.
4 Lightly flour rolling pin and pastry board.
5 Roll pastry to required thickness and shape, lifting and turning to keep it light.
6 Cooking times are given for individual recipes, but as a general rule it should be cooked in a hot oven (425–450°F. – Gas Mark 6–7).

Rich short crust pastry

you will need:

8 oz. flour	1 egg yolk
good pinch salt	cold water to mix
5 oz. fat	

Bake at a slightly lower heat than for short crust pastry (i.e. 400–425°F. – Gas Mark 5–6). (Make as for short crust pastry above.)

Note

This can be used in any recipe where short crust pastry is given, but it is more difficult to roll and handle. It is also less suitable for dishes you intend to carry on a picnic as it is so crumbly and rich.

Flaky pastry

you will need:

8 oz. plain flour	5–6 oz. fat
pinch salt	(½ margarine, ½ lard)
	water to mix

1 Sieve flour with salt.
2 Divide fat into 3 portions.
3 Rub 1 portion into flour in usual way and mix to rolling consistency with cold water.
4 Roll out to oblong shape.
5 Take second portion of fat and divide it into small pieces.
6 Lay pieces of fat on surface of two-thirds of dough, leaving remaining third without fat.
7 Take its 2 corners and fold back over second third so that dough looks like an envelope with its flap open.
8 Fold over to end of pastry closing the 'envelope'.
9 Turn it at right angles, seal open ends of pastry and 'rib' it by depressing with the rolling pin at intervals to give corrugated effect and equalising the pressure of air.
10 This ensures that pastry will rise evenly.
11 Repeat process again using remaining fat and turning pastry in same way.
12 Roll out pastry once more, but should it begin to feel soft and sticky put it into a cold place for 30 minutes to become firm before rolling out.
13 Fold pastry as before, turn it, seal edges and 'rib' it.
14 Altogether the pastry should have 3 foldings and 3 rollings.
15 Stand in a cold place for a little while before baking, since the contrast between the cold and the heat of the oven makes pastry rise better.
16 Use a very hot oven (475°F. – Gas Mark 8) for first 15 minutes.
17 Lower the Gas Mark to 5–6 or turn the electric oven off to cook for remaining time at a lower temperature.

Cheese pastry

you will need:

2 oz. plain flour	1½ oz. cheese, finely
salt	grated
1½ oz. butter or	seasoning
margarine	egg yolk or milk to
	mix

1 Sieve flour and salt.
2 Rub the butter or margarine into the flour.
3 Add the cheese and plenty of seasoning.
4 Make to a firm dough with egg yolk or milk.
5 Always bake cheese pastry in a really hot oven (450°F. – Gas Mark 7) and cool for a few minutes on baking trays as it is very brittle.

Hot water crust pastry (raised pastry*)

you will need:

12 oz. plain flour
pinch salt
3–4 oz. fat
¼ pint water

*this is the recipe which is used for raised pies

1 Sieve flour and salt.
2 Melt fat in warm water and add to flour.
3 Mix together with a knife.
4 Knead gently with fingers.
5 Unlike other pastry, this should be used when warm.
6 Bake in moderately hot oven (400°F. – Gas Mark 5).

Rich cheese pastry

you will need:

4 oz. plain flour
salt and cayenne
  pepper
little dry mustard
2½ oz. butter
2 oz. cheese, grated
1 egg yolk

1 Sieve the flour and seasoning together.
2 Rub in the butter.
3 Add the cheese and bind with the egg yolk.
4 If necessary, add a very little water.
5 Roll out firmly.
6 If baking 'blind' use a hot oven (450°F. – Gas Mark 7), or as directed in the recipe you wish to follow.

Note

Handle carefully when hot since it is very light

Potato pastry

you will need:

3 oz. cooking fat
4 oz. flour
seasoning
4 oz. potatoes, mashed
very little water

1 Rub cooking fat into seasoned flour.
2 Add potatoes.
3 Knead firmly and add only enough water to give firm dough.

Note

This is an excellent pastry for hot savoury dishes.

Puff pastry

you will need:

8 oz. plain flour
good pinch salt
cold water to mix
few drops lemon juice
7–8 oz. fat*

*use ⅔ table margarine and ⅓ light cooking fat

1 Sieve flour and salt together.
2 Mix to rolling consistency with cold water and lemon juice.
3 Roll to oblong shape.
4 Make fat into neat block and place in centre of pastry and fold over it first the bottom section of pastry, then the top section so that fat is quite covered.
5 Turn the dough at right angles, seal edges and 'rib' carefully (see recipe for flaky pastry, page 70).
6 Roll out.
7 Fold dough into envelope, turn, seal edges, 'rib' and roll again.
8 Repeat 5 times, so making 7 rollings and 7 foldings in all.
9 It will be necessary to put pastry to rest in cold place once or twice between rollings to prevent it becoming sticky and soft.
10 Always put it to rest before rolling for the last time.
11 Bake in a very hot oven for the first 10–15 minutes (475–500°F. – Gas Mark 8–9).
12 Lower to Gas Mark 5–6 or turn electric oven right out to finish cooking at lower temperature.

To make vol-au-vent cases

Method 1

1 Roll out puff pastry until just under ½ inch thick.
2 Cut into rounds.
3 From half the rounds make a ring by cutting out centre.
4 Place circle on top of complete round.
5 Seal edges and put on to a damp baking tray or trays.
6 Glaze with beaten egg.
7 Cook as for puff pastry (see above).

Method 2

1 Roll out puff pastry until a good ¾–1 inch thick.
2 Cut into rounds or required shape.
3 Put on to damp baking trays. *continued*

4 With a small cutter press half way through pastry.

5 Glaze with beaten egg.

6 Cook as for puff pastry (see page 71).

7 When cooked remove centre portion with a sharp knife and return to oven for a short time to dry out.

Fillings for vol-au-vent cases

Devilled egg filling – chop hard-boiled eggs and mix with a very small amount of curry powder, chutney and just enough mayonnaise (see page 57) to give soft texture.

Garnish with sliced olives.

Savoury beef filling – fry a small sliced onion and a small skinned tomato until soft. Add 3 oz. finely chopped or minced cooked beef, 1 teaspoon horseradish sauce and enough white sauce or mayonnaise (see pages 57, 83) to moisten.

Scrambled egg and anchovy filling – add 2 tablespoons milk to each egg. Scramble eggs lightly (see page 40). Remove pan from the heat when egg is still very soft and creamy.

Add chopped anchovies. Pile into cases and decorate with curled anchovy fillets.

Savoury sardine filling – mash sardines. Add a squeeze of lemon juice, good pinch of cayenne pepper, salt and mix with chopped whites of hard-boiled egg.

Garnish with yolks of egg before serving.

Chicken and mushroom filling – fry 4 oz. mushrooms in 2 oz. margarine until quite soft. Stir in 1 oz. flour and proceed as for creamed chicken below.

Creamed cheese filling – make a thick sauce of 1 oz. margarine, 1 oz. flour and ¼ pint milk. Season well, then stir in 4 oz. grated or finely chopped cheese. Heat gently, adding 2 tablespoons cream. Mix with chopped gherkins and capers if liked.

Creamed chicken filling

cooking time: about 10 minutes

you will need:

1 oz. margarine	seasoning
1 oz. flour	2 teacups chopped
¾ cup chicken stock	chicken
¾ cup milk	

1 Make a white sauce with the margarine, flour, chicken stock, milk and plenty of seasoning (see page 83).

2 When thickened, stir in the chopped chicken.

3 For picnic vol-au-vent, use only ½ cup each of stock and milk to give a more firm sauce.

4 Keep filling hot and pastry hot, and put together at the last minute.

Corn tartlets

cooking time: 15 minutes

you will need:

4–5 oz. short or cheese pastry (see pages 70, 71)	1 oz. Parmesan cheese **or** Cheddar cheese, grated
4–5 oz. sweet corn	little cream **or** top of milk
2 Demi-sel cheeses*	seasoning
	tomato to garnish

*or 4 oz. cream cheese

1 Line small patty tins with the pastry and bake 'blind' until crisp and golden brown.

2 Mix corn with all other ingredients – saving a little for garnish.

3 Pile into tartlet cases.

4 Either serve cold or reheat gently.

5 Top with corn and butterflies made of tomato.

Variation

Corn and ham tartlets – use 2 oz. finely chopped ham and only 2 oz. cream cheese.

Sardine and tomato squares

cooking time: 25–30 minutes

you will need for 2 servings:

4 oz. short crust or flaky pastry (see page 70)	1 small can sardines (preferably in oil)
2 tomatoes	seasoning

1 Roll out pastry and cut into 2 oblong shapes, exactly the same size.

2 Put 1 piece of pastry on to an ungreased baking tin.

3 Skin both tomatoes and slice thinly.

4 Cover pastry with 1 tomato and with drained, mashed, seasoned sardines.

5 Cover with 2nd sliced tomato and finally with pastry.

6 Press this down firmly. See no fish or tomato is likely to squeeze out during cooking as it would burn.

7 Brush top pastry with a little milk or egg.

8 Bake in centre of a hot oven (450°F. – Gas Mark 7). After 15 minutes the heat can be reduced slightly if the pastry is browning too much.

9 If using flaky pastry bake at 475°F. – Gas Mark 8, for the first 15 minutes, then reduce the heat as desired.

10 Mark into neat squares while still warm.

Variations

Sausage and tomato squares – use recipe above, but instead of sardines use about 4 oz. sausage meat. This is a change from sausage rolls and will be appreciated by people who do not like to eat a lot of pastry.

Salmon and mushroom squares – use recipe above, but use 4 oz. flaked canned salmon instead of sardines. Add 2 oz. chopped mushrooms, tossed in 1 oz. butter or margarine instead of the tomato.

Tuna and tomato squares – use recipe for sardine and tomato squares, but use 4 oz. flaked canned tuna instead of sardines and blend this with 1 oz. grated cheese.

White fish, mushroom and tomato squares – use recipe for sardine and tomato squares but substitute 4 oz. well-drained flaked cooked white fish for the sardines. 1–2 oz. chopped mushrooms, tossed in ½ oz. butter or margarine, should be mixed with the fish to give added flavour.

Prawn and egg patties

cooking time: 15–25 minutes

you will need:

5–6 oz. short crust pastry (see page 70)	2–3 hard-boiled eggs
½ pint white sauce (see page 83)	4 oz. picked prawns parsley lemon juice seasoning

1 Roll out pastry.

2 Line patty tins or large pie plate with pastry

and bake 'blind' for 15 minutes for small tartlets and 25 minutes for large one.

3 Fill with a white sauce in which is a mixture of chopped hard-boiled eggs, prawns, little chopped parsley, lemon juice and seasoning to taste.

Variations

Shrimp and egg patties – use previous recipe but use 4 oz. shrimps in place of the prawns.

Salmon egg patties – use previous recipe but use 4–6 oz. flaked canned or cooked salmon and 1 tablespoon finely diced cucumber as well as the eggs.

Beef shells

cooking time: 2 hours

you will need:

6 oz. short crust pastry (see page 70)	just under ⅓ pint steak stock (if using stewing steak), for rump steak use water and little meat extract to flavour
1 onion	
1 oz. dripping	
12 oz. rump steak, or stewing steak, diced or minced	
8 oz. tomatoes	1 teaspoon Worcestershire sauce
¾ oz. flour	
1 teaspoon curry powder	seasoning little mashed potato

1 If using stewing steak, simmer gently in water to cover, seasoning well until just tender.

2 Drain and save some of the stock.

3 Ask the fishmonger for large scallop shells.

4 Line these with thin pastry and bake 'blind' until crisp and golden brown.

5 Fry the chopped onion in the dripping.

6 Add the steak, the chopped tomatoes and the flour and curry powder.

7 Cook gently for several minutes.

8 Add the stock and water, bring to the boil and cook until thoroughly smooth and thick.

9 Add the sauce and any extra seasoning desired.

10 Pipe a thin border of soft creamed potato round the edge of each pastry shell, being very careful not to break the pastry.

11 Fill with the beef mixture.

Savoury basket flan

cooking time: 1–1½ hours

you will need:

6 oz. potato pastry
or cheese pastry
(see page 70)

fillings (see below)

1 Roll out the pastry and line a flan ring or tin –
   fairly shallow about 7 inches in diameter. Save
   a little pastry to make a strip for a handle.
2 Bake for approximately 25 minutes for the
   flan and little less for the 'handle' in a hot oven
   (450°F. – Gas Mark 7).
3 Put in the filling and place handle into position.

Filling 1

12 oz. cooked
   mixed vegetables

½ pint thick cheese
   sauce (see page 83)
1 hard-boiled egg

1 Strain vegetables and stir into the sauce.
2 Garnish with egg and serve hot.

Filling 2

2 onions
little fat
1 can tomatoes
12 oz. minced
   beef

seasoning
chopped parsley
parsley to garnish

1 Cut the onions into rings and fry in the fat until
   tender.
2 Lift out half the onions.
3 Add the can of tomatoes to the rest of the onion
   and the beef and simmer gently, stirring well to
   break up the beef, until tender (about 45
   minutes) and thick. Season well.
4 Garnish with parsley and the onion rings.
5 Serve hot or cold.

Filling 3

1 medium sized can
   salmon
2 or 3 hard-boiled
   eggs

¼ pint thick white
   sauce (see page 83)
sliced tomatoes

1 Add salmon to sauce, together with 1 or 2
   chopped eggs.
2 Garnish with egg and tomato and serve hot or
   cold.

Bacon twists

cooking time: 30–35 minutes

you will need:

10 oz. short crust
   pastry (see page
   70)
4–6 rashers
   streaky bacon

1 oz. margarine
1 good sized onion,
   finely chopped
pinch sage
seasoning

1 Roll out the pastry into a neat oblong shape.
2 Cut into 2 equal sized pieces.
3 Chop bacon very finely and fry until golden
   brown.
4 Lift out of pan, add margarine.
5 Fry onion in this.
6 Add to bacon with sage and seasoning.
7 Spread over one half of the pastry, cover with
   the second oblong of pastry.
8 Cut into strips then twist these in centre.
9 Lift on to baking tins and bake for about 25
   minutes in hot oven (425–450°F. – Gas Mark
   6–7).

Savoury soufflé tarts

cooking time: 15 minutes

you will need:

6 oz. short crust
   pastry (see page 70)

for filling:

1 onion, chopped
2 large or 3 small
   eggs
pinch mixed herbs

2–3 oz. cheese, finely
   grated
seasoning

1 Line 9–12 fairly deep patty tins with pastry.
2 Soak the onion in about 1 tablespoon water for
   a while.
3 Mix with the other ingredients.
4 Put spoonfuls of the egg mixture into pastry
   cases and bake in a moderately hot oven
   (400°F. – Gas Mark 5).
5 Serve hot or cold.

Variations

Ham soufflé tarts – use 2 oz. very finely chopped
cooked ham and 1 oz. grated cheese instead of
all cheese. Parmesan cheese is ideal in this
recipe.

Mushroom soufflé tarts – fry 2 oz. finely chopped
mushrooms in ½–1 oz. butter, add to eggs with
1 oz. grated cheese. Parmesan cheese is ideal in
this recipe.

Cheese and vegetable flan

cooking time: 1 hour

you will need:

for cheese pastry:

4 oz. flour	2 oz. cheese, grated
2 oz. margarine or cooking fat	seasoning
	egg yolk or water

for the filling:

1 small onion	seasoning
knob butter	2 eggs
3 good sized tomatoes	2 oz. cheese, grated
	⅛ pint milk
1 or 2 mushrooms (optional)	1 carrot, grated

1 Line deep flan ring or tin with the pastry.
2 Chop the onion finely and fry until soft, but not browned, in the butter.
3 Slice the tomatoes and chop the mushrooms.
4 Mix with the onion and put at the bottom of the flan case, seasoning this layer well.
5 Mix together the eggs, cheese, milk, seasoning, add the grated carrot and pour over the tomato layer.
6 Bake in the centre of a moderately hot oven (400°F. – Gas Mark 5) for about 25 minutes.
7 Lower the heat to very moderate (350°F. – Gas Mark 3) for a further 25–30 minutes until the filling feels firm.
8 Serve hot or cold.

Quiche Lorraine

cooking time: 45–55 minutes

you will need:

3 rashers bacon	just under ⅛ pint milk
6 oz. short crust pastry (see page 70)	⅛ pint thin cream or evaporated milk
	seasoning
2 eggs	4 oz. cheese, grated

1 Chop and fry the bacon until crisp.
2 Line a really deep tin with the pastry.
3 Beat the eggs, add milk, cream, seasoning, bacon and cheese.
4 Pour carefully into the flan case.
5 Bake in the centre of a moderately hot oven (400°F. – Gas Mark 5) until pastry is cooked and filling is set.

Variations

Special occasion quiche – use flaky instead of short crust pastry and half cream and half milk. Increase the amount of cheese.

Economical quiche – use egg yolks only, saving the whites for meringues or another dish. Use all milk.

Vegetable quiche – use diced cooked vegetables instead of bacon. Make sure these are only lightly cooked and not watery, otherwise they are not very appetising in the flan.

Mushroom and prawn quiche

cooking time: 50 minutes

you will need:

4–5 oz. short crust pastry (see page 70)	2 eggs
2–4 oz. mushrooms	2–4 oz. prawns
little butter	⅛ pint milk
	2 oz. cheese, grated
	seasoning

for garnish:

parsley, chopped	spinach, cooked and chopped
prawns	

1 Line flan ring or sandwich tin with pastry.
2 Bake 'blind' in hot oven for 10 minutes only.
3 Slice and fry mushrooms in butter and put at bottom of flan.
4 Beat eggs, add most of the prawns, chopped in pieces, leaving largest for garnish, the milk, cheese and seasoning. Pour over mushrooms.
5 Bake for approximately 35–40 minutes in centre of moderate oven (375°F. – Gas Mark 4).
6 Garnish with parsley or spinach and prawns.
7 Serve hot or cold.

Savoury custard flan

cooking time: 35 minutes

you will need:

6 oz. short crust pastry (see page 70)	few cooked mixed vegetables (peas, sliced carrots, beetroot, etc.)
2 eggs	
⅛ pint milk	
seasoning	3 oz. cheese, grated

1 Line a 7-inch flan ring or sandwich tin with pastry and bake 'blind' in the middle of a hot oven (450°F. – Gas Mark 7) for 10 minutes.
2 Beat the eggs and pour on the milk.
3 Season well.
4 Arrange the vegetables in the flan case.
5 Pour the custard carefully over them, and sprinkle cheese on top.
6 Bake in the middle of a moderate oven.(375–400°F. – Gas Mark 4–5) for approximately 25 minutes until the custard is set.

Egg and bacon flan

cooking time: 35 minutes

you will need:

5–6 oz. short crust pastry (see page 70)	4–6 oz. bacon, diced 3 or 4 eggs seasoning

1 Line flan tin with pastry and bake for about 10 minutes to set, but not cook, the pastry.
2 Fry the diced bacon until just crisp.
3 Add this to the well-beaten and seasoned eggs.
4 Pour the mixture into the flan case.
5 Set for a further 25 minutes in a moderately hot oven.

Variation

Egg and bacon pie – use ingredients as above, but use 10 oz. pastry. Line tin with half the pastry, then put in the filling, using the larger quantity of bacon and eggs. Cover with pastry, seal edges, make slit on top for steam to escape. Bake for approximately 25 minutes in a hot oven (425–450°F. – Gas Mark 6–7) until pastry is set and brown, then lower the heat to moderate (400°F. – Gas Mark 5) for a further 20 minutes.

Egg and mushroom flan

cooking time: 45 minutes

you will need:

3 oz. mushrooms 1 oz. butter 3 eggs ⅛ pint milk **or** cream seasoning	5–6 oz. short crust pastry (see page 70) 2 oz. cheese, grated

1 Cook the mushrooms (chopped if liked) in the butter.
2 Put into a basin.
3 Add the eggs, cream or milk and season well.
4 Pour into flan case and top with the cheese.
5 Cook in moderately hot oven for approximately 30–35 minutes until pastry is crisp and the filling is set.

Variation

Egg and mushroom pie – use ingredients as before, but use 10 oz. short crust pastry. Line tin with half the pastry, mixing the cheese with the eggs to make a filling.
Cover with pastry, seal edges, make slit on top for steam to escape.

Bake for approximately 25 minutes in a hot oven (425–450°F. – Gas Mark 6–7) until pastry is set and brown. Lower heat to moderate (400°F. – Gas Mark 5) for a further 20 minutes.

Egg and spinach pie

cooking time: 40 minutes

you will need:

8 oz. short crust pastry (see page 70) 1 lb. cooked spinach purée 4 eggs	seasoning 1 oz. butter 2–3 tablespoons cream little milk

1 Use half the pastry to line a pie plate or flan ring – the pastry should be very thin.
2 Cover with the spinach purée and then make a slight 'well' in this for each of the 4 eggs.
3 Break eggs carefully into the 'wells'
4 Season and put on the butter and cream.
5 Cover with the rest of the pastry, brush with a little milk and make air holes for the steam to escape.
6 Bake for approximately 40 minutes in the centre of a moderately hot oven (400°F. – Gas Mark 5).
7 Serve hot or cold.

Chicken shortcakes

cooking time: 20 minutes

you will need:

for chicken filling:

4 oz. mushrooms 3 oz. butter 2 oz. plain flour ½ pint chicken stock ½ pint milk 8–12 oz. cooked chicken	2 tablespoons chopped red pepper (optional) seasoning to taste

shortcakes:

12 oz. flour (with plain flour 4 level teaspoons baking powder, 1 level teaspoon baking powder with self-raising flour)	½ level teaspoon salt 3 oz. butter milk to mix milk or beaten egg for glazing

1 Fry chopped mushrooms in butter.
2 Stir in flour and cook for several minutes.
3 Gradually add the stock and milk, bringing to the boil until thickened.
4 Add remaining ingredients and season to taste.

5 Cover pan and keep hot until ready to serve.

Shortcakes:

6 Sift together flour, baking powder and salt then rub in fat.

7 Add the milk and mix to form a soft dough.

8 Knead very lightly on a floured board and roll out to about 1 inch in thickness.

9 Cut into 4–6 rounds of 3–3½ inches in diameter and brush tops with milk or beaten egg.

10 Bake towards the top of a hot oven (450°F. – Gas Mark 7) for 15–20 minutes.

11 Remove from oven and carefully break short-cakes in half.

12 Spoon hot chicken filling over bottom halves, place on tops and serve at once.

Tomato and onion pie

cooking time: 40 minutes

you will need:

2–3 onions	seasoning
4–5 oz. short crust	paprika pepper
pastry (see page 70)	4 oz. cream cheese
3–4 tomatoes	2 eggs

1 Slice or chop onions and simmer gently in boiling salted water until soft.

2 Drain, but keep just a little of the stock.

3 Line pie plate with pastry.

4 Cover with skinned and thinly sliced tomatoes and onions, season.

5 Beat cream cheese and eggs – season well.

6 Gradually beat in 1 tablespoon stock to make a smooth mixture.

7 Pour over onions and tomatoes and bake in the centre of a moderate oven (375°F. – Gas Mark 4).

Tomato tart

cooking time: 35–40 minutes

you will need:

small onion	pinch salt
4 large tomatoes	pepper
2 oz. butter	pinch sugar
little milk	1 pastry flan case*
slice bread	2–3 oz. cheese,
4–8 oz. cooked	grated
ham, chopped	

*bake until just brown.

1 Fry the sliced onion and tomatoes gently in the butter.

2 Meanwhile, pour enough milk over the bread (crust removed) to soften it, then beat well.

3 Add this to the cooked tomatoes and onion, together with the ham, and season well. Add the sugar.

4 Put in the flan case.

5 Cover with a layer of thick grated cheese.

6 Put into the oven for a short time to melt the cheese.

Quick Toasted Snacks

Toasted snacks are so easy and can be extremely appetising as well. They can be anything from a main meal to a dainty titbit to tempt the appetite.

10 savoury spreads for toast or sandwiches

1 **Grated cheese,** grated carrot and a little chopped parsley, mixed together with mayonnaise.

2 **Creamed butter,** chopped watercress and a squeeze of lemon juice, seasoned well.

3 **Creamed cheese** and finely chopped **celery,** garnished with green leaves.

4 **Creamed cheese** and chopped boiled **bacon** or ham, with just a touch of chutney.

5 Chopped **hard-boiled eggs,** crisp chopped bacon and little mayonnaise to bind.

6 Chopped **soft-boiled eggs,** knob butter, little chopped parsley or watercress, pinch celery salt and seasoning.

7 Chopped **hard-boiled eggs,** pinch **curry powder** and a little chutney.

8 **Chopped tongue,** chopped beetroot and little mayonnaise to bind.

9 **Flaked cooked haddock,** chopped lettuce and chopped gherkin – with butter to bind.

10 **Flaked cooked kippers** – be careful to take out all the bones – little butter, squeeze of lemon juice and lots of pepper.

Escallop brochettes

cooking time: 10 minutes

you will need:

bacon rashers	toast
escallops	

1 Roll rashers of bacon round escallops and grill steadily.
2 Serve on rounds of hot toast.

Cream herring roes

cooking time: 10 minutes

you will need:

herring roes	toast
little milk and	cayenne or paprika
cream	pepper
salt	parsley

1 Simmer the herring roes in a very little milk and cream, adding little salt.
2 Drain well and serve on hot buttered toast, garnishing with cayenne or paprika pepper and parsley.

Smoked haddock pyramids

cooking time: few minutes

you will need:

8 oz. cooked	1 oz. butter
smoked haddock,	1 egg
flaked	1 oz. cheese, grated
1–2 tablespoons	toast
milk or cream	parsley

1 Heat haddock in a saucepan with milk or cream, butter, egg and cheese.
2 Pile on to rounds of toast in a pyramid shape and garnish with chopped parsley.

Crispy herring roes

cooking time: 10 minutes

you will need:

herring roes	fat for frying
egg white	toast
crisp breadcrumbs	paprika or cayenne
cheese, grated	pepper
	parsley

1 Coat herring roes with a little beaten egg white, crisp crumbs and grated cheese.
2 Fry until golden brown and serve on hot toast.
3 Garnish with paprika or cayenne pepper and parsley.

Kipper toasts

cooking time: 16 minutes

you will need:

3 large or 4 small	1 oz. margarine
kippers	4 slices buttered
pepper	toast

1 The best way of cooking kippers is to pour boiling water over the kippers and leave for about 15 minutes. Flake the fish when cooked.
2 Mix the flesh with pepper (no salt) and the margarine.
3 Spread on the hot toast and grill for about 1 minute.

Variation

Kipper toast and egg – prepare the kipper toasts as above, but before spreading on the toast mix with a well-beaten egg, heat gently in a pan and when the egg is set pile on toast. Do not brown under the grill.

Kipper cheese spread

cooking time: 5 minutes

1 Mix equal quantities of grated cheese and flaked cooked kipper flesh together.
2 Spread on hot toast, put under grill for a few minutes and garnish with pats of parsley mixed with butter.

Prawn butter

cooking time: 5 minutes

1 Work 3 oz. chopped prawns into approximately 1½ oz. butter.
2 Add little chopped parsley and squeeze lemon juice.
3 Spread on to very hot toast.
4 Cut into fingers.

Salmon mornay

cooking time: 10 minutes

1 Cover slices of hot buttered toast with flaked tinned salmon.
2 Add slices of cheese or a thick layer of grated cheese or a thick cheese sauce (see page 83).
3 Brown steadily under the grill.

Prawn and grapefruit slices

cooking time: 10 minutes

Arrange peeled prawns and sections of fresh grapefruit on hot buttered toast, brush with melted butter and heat for a few minutes under grill.

Devilled sardines

cooking time: 5 minutes

you will need:

2 oz. butter	toast
pinch curry powder and mustard	1 can sardines
little Worcestershire sauce	crisp breadcrumbs

1 Cream the butter. Add pinch curry powder, mustard and a few drops Worcestershire sauce.
2 Spread over 2–3 slices of toast.
3 Arrange drained sardines on the toast, then sprinkle crisp crumbs over sardines and heat under grill.

Tuna mornay

cooking time: 10 minutes

1 Blend flaked tuna fish with a little oil, seasoning, and a very little grated onion or chopped chives.
2 Spread on hot buttered toast.
3 Cover with grated cheese or thin slices of cheese or a thick cheese sauce (see page 83).
4 Brown steadily under the grill.

Toasted bacon sandwiches

Toasted bacon sandwiches are made by putting crisp rashers of bacon between slices of toast, but they can be varied in a number of ways:

With cheese – put a slice of cheese with the hot bacon and return under the grill for a few minutes to allow cheese to melt slightly.

With chutney – spread the toast with butter and chutney, then put in the grilled rashers of bacon.

With egg – top one slice of buttered toast with crisp grilled bacon rashers and a fried egg, top with a second slice of crisp toast.

With prunes – put a few stoned cooked prunes over the hot toast, cover with the crisp bacon rashers and a second slice of toast.

With liver pâté – spread the hot toast with liver pâté, then with bacon rashers and more toast.

Scrambled rice and bacon

cooking time: 12 minutes

you will need:

4 rashers bacon	3 eggs
3 tablespoons milk	seasoning
3 good tablespoons cooked rice	4 slices bread
	1 oz. butter

1 Chop the bacon into tiny pieces.
2 Put into a saucepan and cook until crisp and golden.
3 Add milk and rice and heat for a few minutes.
4 Stir in beaten and seasoned eggs.
5 Cook gently until the eggs have set and put on to slices of hot buttered toast.

Jamaican sausages

cooking time: 3–5 minutes

you will need:

sausages, grilled	halved pineapple
buttered toast	rings
French mustard	lettuce

1 Put grilled sausages on to hot buttered toast.
2 Spread with little French mustard.
3 Arrange halved rings pineapple over sausages.
4 Garnish with lettuce.

Swiss toasts

cooking time: 5–8 minutes

you will need:

buttered toast	Gruyère cheese
cooked ham	tomato
chutney	

1 Spread slices of hot toast with butter.
2 Cover each piece of toast with a slice of cooked ham, little chutney and a slice of Gruyère cheese.
3 Garnish with rings of tomato and heat for a few minutes under the grill or in the oven.

Cheese and sardine fingers

cooking time: 10 minutes

you will need:

1 small can sardines in oil	2 oz. Cheddar cheese, grated
seasoning	little margarine or butter if necessary
1 oz. breadcrumbs	4 slices buttered toast
½ teaspoon made mustard	1 tomato
1 teaspoon Worcestershire sauce	

1 Mash the sardines very well and season.
2 Mix the oil from the can of sardines with the breadcrumbs, seasoning, Worcestershire sauce and cheese. If there is not sufficient oil to give a soft mixture, then add a little margarine or butter and cream well.
3 Spread the mashed sardines on the slices of toast and cover with the crumb mixture.

4 Put under a hot grill for a few minutes until crisp and golden brown.
5 Garnish with a small piece of tomato. Serve hot or cold. If serving hot, they can be prepared earlier and just heated in oven.

Cheese and apple are a perfect combination and they will give you a new snack in a very few minutes.

Cheddar surprise

cooking time: 5–8 minutes

1 Peel and core fairly sweet apples.
2 Fry thick rings of apple in bacon fat or butter.
3 When apples are soft, add slices of Cheddar cheese and leave in fat until beginning to melt.
4 Put apple rings covered with cheese slices on to hot buttered toast.

Cheesy scramble

cooking time: 5–8 minutes

you will need:

little butter	4 slices toast
4 oz. cream cheese	little parsley or
4 eggs	chives, chopped,
seasoning	when available

1 Put a knob of butter into a saucepan and add the cream cheese and the well-beaten and seasoned eggs.
2 Stir together **very slowly** until the eggs are set.
3 Meanwhile toast the bread, butter it and cover with the egg mixture.
4 Garnish with chopped parsley or chives.

English monkey

cooking time: 10 minutes

you will need:

1 oz. butter	1 egg
¼ pint milk	seasoning
2 oz. soft	mustard
breadcrumbs	Worcestershire sauce
4 oz. cheese,	4 slices toast
grated	tomato

1 Heat the butter in a pan.
2 Add milk and breadcrumbs.
3 When very hot add grated cheese and beaten egg.
4 Season well, adding little made mustard and a few drops Worcestershire sauce.
5 Stir together until thick and creamy.
6 Pour on to toast.
7 Garnish with sliced tomato.

Golden cheese fingers

cooking time: 5 minutes

you will need:

2 medium sized raw	few drops tomato
carrots	ketchup
6 oz. cheese, grated	seasoning
2 oz. butter or	4 slices bread
margarine	tomatoes

1 Grate carrots and mix with 5 oz. of the cheese, 1½ oz. of the butter, the tomato ketchup and seasoning.
2 Toast bread and spread with rest of butter.
3 Pile cheese and carrot mixture on toast.
4 Sprinkle with rest of cheese and brown under grill.
5 Garnish with grilled tomatoes.

Apple rarebit

cooking time: 5 minutes

you will need:

4 slices bread	little butter
4 dessert apple rings	

for cheese topping:

4 oz. grated cheese	little seasoning
1 oz. butter	1 tablespoon milk
¼ teaspoon made	
mustard	

1 Put the bread on the grid of the grill pan to toast, and spread the slices of apple with a little butter and toast at the same time.

2 When the bread is crisp, butter and put the apple rings on top.
3 Blend the cheese with the butter, mustard, seasoning and milk.
4 Spread over the toast, trying to cover the apple rings.
5 Return to the grill to melt the cheese.
6 Serve at once.

Celery rarebit

cooking time: 12 minutes

you will need:

1 medium sized	3–4 slices bread
can celery hearts	butter

for cheese topping:

1 oz. margarine or	little made mustard
butter	celery salt
1 oz. flour	6–8 oz. cheese, grated
salt	few drops
pepper	Worcestershire
	sauce

1 Drain liquid from can of celery and, if necessary, add enough milk to make up to ¼ pint.
2 Make a thick white sauce with margarine, flour and celery liquid (see page 83).
3 Add seasoning, grated cheese and sauce.
4 Spread toast with butter, put celery hearts on top.
5 Heat for a few minutes under the grill.
6 Cover with the rarebit mixture and return to grill to brown.

Variation
With ale – a few drops of ale may be added instead of the sauce.

Soufflé rarebit

cooking time: 7 minutes

you will need:

3 eggs	1 tablespoon cream
4 oz. cheese, finely	seasoning
grated	4 slices toast

1 Beat yolks of eggs with cheese, cream and seasoning.
2 Fold the stiffly beaten whites of the eggs into the mixture.
3 Spread on to hot buttered toast.
4 Heat under moderate grill until golden brown.

Mexican rarebit

cooking time: 12 minutes

you will need:

1 onion	2 oz. diced cooked
2 tomatoes,	vegetables
skinned	2 eggs
2 oz. margarine	seasoning
4–6 oz. cheese,	4 slices toast
grated	little extra margarine
	or butter

1 Chop onion and tomatoes finely and fry in the hot margarine.
2 Add the cheese, vegetables and beaten eggs.
3 Season and heat gently until cheese has melted and eggs set.
4 Toast bread and butter.
5 Pile cheese mixture on top.

Spinach mornay

cooking time: 20–25 minutes

Soft creamed spinach is a good contrast to crisp toast.

1 Cook fresh or frozen spinach until tender, chop and mix with a little butter, cream and seasoning.
2 Put on top of thin crisp buttered toast.
3 Cover with a thick layer of grated cheese and heat for a few minutes under a hot grill.

Italian toast topping

cooking time: 12–15 minutes

you will need:

slices bread	butter

for topping:

1 medium onion	2 tablespoons cooking
1 medium green	oil
pepper	2 eggs
4 medium tomatoes	seasoning to taste
1 aubergine	
(approximately 4 oz.)	

1 Peel and chop the onion.
2 Chop the pepper finely – removing all seeds.
3 Skin and chop tomatoes.

4 Slice but do not peel aubergine.
5 Sauté vegetables in the hot oil for 5–7 minutes.
6 Add eggs, season.
7 Cook gently, stirring, until eggs are just set.
8 Serve over toast triangles.
9 Serve with pickled cabbage, radishes and spring onions, strips of peeled cucumber.

Savoury celery rarebit

cooking time: 25–30 minutes

you will need:

1 medium sized stick	Ingredients for
celery or can celery	Welsh rarebit
hearts	(see right)
4 slices toast	

1 Cut the celery into neat pieces.
2 Cook in boiling salted water until just soft.
3 Arrange on the hot pieces of toast and put the rarebit mixture on top.
4 Put under a hot grill to brown.

Mushroom and kidney scramble

cooking time: 13 minutes

you will need:

2 kidneys	3 eggs
4 large mushrooms	1 tablespoon cream
1½ oz. butter	toast
seasoning	butter or liver pâté
mixed herbs	

1 Fry the sliced kidneys and sliced mushrooms in the butter.
2 Season well and add pinch mixed herbs.
3 When tender add eggs, beaten with the cream.
4 Scramble slightly.
5 Serve on toast spread with butter or liver pâté.

Welsh rarebit

cooking time: 10 minutes

you will need:

1 oz. butter or margarine	mustard
½ oz. flour	1 tablespoon beer or ale
¼ pint milk	6 oz. cheese, grated
seasoning	toast

1 Melt margarine in pan, stir in flour and cook until roux is dry.

2 Add cold milk, bring to the boil and cook until very thick.

3 Season well, adding beer or ale and nearly all the cheese.

4 Spread on hot toast, sprinkle remainder of cheese on top.

5 Brown under hot grill.

Variation

With sauce – instead of beer, use 1 dessert-spoon Worcestershire sauce.

Sauces

White sauce

cooking time: 5–8 minutes

you will need:

1 oz. butter or margarine	½ pint milk for thick coating sauce **or** 1 pint milk for thin white sauce **or** ¼ pint milk for panada, for binding
1 oz. flour	
salt and pepper	

1 Heat the butter gently.

2 Remove from the heat and stir in the flour.

3 Return to the heat and cook gently for a few minutes, so that the roux, as the butter and flour mixture is called, does not brown.

4 Add milk, bring to the boil and cook, stirring with a wooden spoon, until smooth and thickened.

5 Season well.

6 If any lumps have formed, whisk sharply.

Variations

Cheese sauce – use method for white sauce, but stir in 3–6 oz. grated cheese when sauce has thickened. Add mustard.

Parsley sauce – use method for white sauce, but add 1–2 teaspoons chopped parsley.

Béchamel sauce – use method for white sauce but infuse a piece each of very finely chopped onion, carrot and celery in the milk. Strain this and use where milk is used in the recipe.

Prawn or shrimp sauce – use method for white sauce (see left) adding about ⅛–¼ pint chopped prawns and a little anchovy essence just before serving. If using fresh prawns, simmer shells and use ¼ pint stock instead of the same amount of milk.

Mushroom sauce – use method for white sauce (see left) but simmer 2–4 oz. chopped mushrooms in the milk until tender. Use this in the white sauce.

Onion sauce – use method for white sauce (see left) but boil 3 onions, chop or slice and add these to the sauce. Use little onion stock in place of milk if liked.

Brown sauce

(coating consistency)

you will need:

1 oz. cooking fat or dripping	½ pint brown stock
1 oz. flour	salt and pepper

1 Make as for white sauce (see page 83).
2 For a better flavour fry a little chopped onion and other vegetables in the dripping or fat first, using 2 oz. of this.
3 Strain if wished.

Hollandaise sauce

cooking time: 20–30 minutes

you will need:

2 egg yolks	1–2 tablespoons lemon juice or white wine vinegar
pinch cayenne pepper	
salt	2–4 oz. butter

1 Put the egg yolks, seasonings and vinegar into the top of a double saucepan.
2 Whisk over hot water until sauce begins to thicken.
3 Add the butter in very small pieces, whisking in each pat and allowing it to melt before adding the next.
4 **Do not allow to boil as it will curdle.**
5 If too thick, add a little cream.

Economical Hollandaise sauce

cooking time: 10–15 minutes

1 Make a white sauce (see page 83).
2 Remove from heat and whisk in 1 egg, 1 dessertspoon lemon juice or vinegar.
3 Cook gently without boiling for a few minutes.

Tartare sauce

There are several ways of making this:

Use the **Hollandaise sauce** as a basis, and add 1 tablespoon chopped gherkins, 1 dessertspoon chopped capers and 1 dessertspoon chopped parsley.
Use the **Economical Hollandaise sauce** as a basis and add above ingredients to this, increasing the amounts slightly.
Use **mayonnaise** as a basis and add gherkins, capers, parsley to this.

Tomato sauce

cooking time: 40 minutes

you will need:

1 carrot	½ oz. flour
1 small onion	¼ pint stock or liquid from can
1 rasher bacon	
1 oz. butter	bay leaf
5 oz. large fresh or canned tomatoes	salt and pepper
	good pinch sugar

1 Dice carrot, onion and bacon.
2 Heat butter and toss them in this – do not brown.
3 Add tomatoes and simmer for a few minutes with canned tomatoes, rather longer with fresh ones. Take time doing this since it improves the flavour of the sauce.
4 Blend flour with stock and add bay leaf.
5 Add to ingredients and simmer gently for about 30 minutes, stirring from time to time.
6 Rub through a sieve or beat with a wooden spoon.
7 Add seasoning and sugar.

Index